Probation and Social Work on Trial

Probation and Social Work on Trial

Violent Offenders and Child Abusers

Wendy Fitzgibbon
London Metropolitan University, UK

First published 2011 by
PALGRAVE MACMILLAN

Palgrave Macmillan in the UK is an imprint of Macmillan Publishers Limited, registered in England, company number 785998, of Houndmills, Basingstoke, Hampshire RG21 6XS.

Palgrave Macmillan in the US is a division of St Martin's Press LLC, 175 Fifth Avenue, New York, NY 10010.

Palgrave Macmillan is the global academic imprint of the above companies and has companies and representatives throughout the world.

Palgrave® and Macmillan® are registered trademarks in the United States, the United Kingdom, Europe and other countries

ISBN 978-0-230-27537-9

This book is printed on paper suitable for recycling and made from fully managed and sustained forest sources. Logging, pulping and manufacturing processes are expected to conform to the environmental regulations of the country of origin.

A catalogue record for this book is available from the British Library.

Library of Congress Cataloging-in-Publication Data
Fitzgibbon, Wendy.
  Probation and social work on trial : violent offenders and child
  abusers / Wendy Fitzgibbon.
     p. cm.
  Includes index.
  ISBN 978-0-230-27537-9 (hardback)
    1. Child abuse—Great Britain. 2. Probation—Great Britain. 3. Family
  violence—Great Britain. I. Title.
  HV6626.54.G7F58 2011
  364.6'30941—dc23   2011024173

Printed and bound in Great Britain by
CPI Antony Rowe, Chippenham and Eastbourne

For Jack and Irene Fitzgibbon

Contents

Acknowledgements

This book would not have been possible without the support, guidance and insight of a number of academics and practitioners. I hope that I have sufficiently recognised and acknowledged the skill and dedication of practitioners working in the demanding areas of probation and child protection services. If I have managed to give a voice to many of their concerns I will have succeeded in one of my aims.

In particular I wish to thank Sharon Brereton, Steven Calder, Angus Cameron, Shirley George, Anthony Goodman, John Harding, Charlotte Holt, John Lea, John Lloyd, Helen Lockwood, Clare Martindale, Julie Olayinka, Janet Ransom, Adrian Smith, Lucien Spencer, Bill Weston and Graham Wheeler. I am as ever indebted to my family and friends for their abundant encouragement and support and their ceaseless faith in this project. Any mistakes or misconceptions are my own.

1
Introduction

In June 2008 Dano Sonnex and his accomplice Nigel Farmer in what the prosecuting counsel at the subsequent trial called a 'joint enterprise of unmitigated evil' brutally tortured and murdered two French research students, Gabriel Ferez and Laurent Bonomo, having broken into their flat in the New Cross area of south London, in an orgy of violence, stabbing the students over 200 times (Gill et al. 2009).

It soon became clear that this was not simply a tragic murder but one that on the face of it could have been prevented: Sonnex was on release from prison on licence and was under the supervision of London Probation (Hill 2009). The fact that the victims were French visitors added to the subsequent media furore. Jack Straw the Justice Secretary made a personal apology to the parents of the victims. He also secured the resignation of David Scott, the Chief of London Probation, who had admitted failings on the part of the service (Bird & Ford 2009).

Sonnex had in fact been under the supposedly watchful eyes of the criminal justice system for some time. Originally sentenced in March 2003 to eight years in prison after pleading guilty to four offences of robbery, he was sent to Aylesbury Young Offender Institution (YOI). The following year he was transferred to the Portland YOI where he told a doctor that 'he could kill'. His record in custody was anything but peaceful. Between March 2003 and May 2006, he had 41 adjudications including eight for violence, eight for drug offences and 13 for breach of rules. He was regarded as constituting a high risk of harm to the public and, unsurprisingly, his application for parole in July 2006 was rejected. In May 2007 he was moved to Elmley jail on the Isle of Sheppey where, in September of that year, his second parole application was refused (Hill 2009).

In February 2008 he was released automatically, having served two thirds of his sentence. The release conditions stipulated mandatory supervision by the probation service until October 2008 and his release licence was set to expire in October 2009. Throughout this period he was considered at risk of recall to prison because of likely re-offending.

On his release he went to live with his mother in New Cross, South London and hardly had he left prison when re-offending began. A matter of weeks after his release he tied up a five-months pregnant woman and her partner, put pillowcases over their heads and demanded money. He turned up regularly for his weekly appointments with his probation officer until the end of April when he was remanded in custody for handling stolen goods and for missing his probation appointment. He was remanded again in custody at the beginning of May, accused of handling stolen goods and, shortly afterwards, his probation officer initiated recall to prison proceedings.

On 16th May 2008 he appeared at Greenwich Magistrates' Court in connection with the stolen goods charge and was released on bail. On 13th June his parole licence was revoked by the Ministry of Justice but there was no immediate action by the police, despite requests from the probation service to apprehend Sonnex for his return to prison. It was on 29th June, 16 days after the revocation of his parole licence, that he and Farmer, fuelled by drink and drugs, burst into the flat occupied by Ferez and Bonomo and subjected the latter to a frenzied attack involving stabbing a total of 244 times during a three-hour torture ordeal. Sonnex and Farmer made off with games consoles, mobile phones and bank cards from which they withdrew £360. They torched the flat and left the fire brigade to find the victims. Sonnex was finally found on 14th July hiding in the loft of his grandparents' home (Wood & Lynch 2009). The trial of Sonnex and Farmer took place at the Old Bailey in June 2009. Sonnex was given a minimum term of 40 years and Farmer 35 years.

The case had an international aspect as it had involved French citizens but from the standpoint of London Probation what made the case all the more serious was the fact that this failure came only four years after the City financier, John Monckton, had been stabbed to death in his Chelsea home in 2004 by Damien Hanson and Elliot

White (HM Inspectorate of Probation 2006b). Hanson, it transpired, was at the time under the supervision of London Probation in much the same way as Sonnex. He had been recently released from custody on licence after completing half of a 12-year sentence for attempted murder and had been assessed as being at low risk of re-offending. As a result of the Hanson case four probation officers were suspended for failure to supervise his licence effectively.

But Sonnex also came close on the heels of another high profile murder in London in which the participants, including in this case the victim, were already known to and under the surveillance of the authorities. In August 2007 a 15-month-old-child, Peter Connelly, hitherto known to the press for reasons of legal anonymity only as 'Baby P.' or later Baby Peter, was found dead in his cot. His mother's boyfriend Steven Barker was convicted together with the latter's brother Jason Owen of causing or allowing the death of a child. Peter's mother, Tracey Connelly, pleaded guilty to the same charge (Department for Education 2010a, 2010b).

This time it was local authority children's services who were in the firing line. Baby Peter (which is the nomenclature I shall adhere to in this book) had at the time of his death been on the child protection register and under the supervision of social workers from the child protection team at the London Borough of Haringey.

The death of such a small and vulnerable child naturally elicited a wave of public sympathy and equally inevitably the media and political spotlight focused on the social workers concerned together with their management. Like the Sonnex case, the matter reached ministerial level with Children's Secretary Ed Balls using his statutory powers to dismiss the head of children's services in Haringey, Sharon Shoesmith. Shoesmith became, as will be seen later, the subject of what to many commentators seemed like a prolonged media witch hunt (Drake 2008).

Peter Connelly was born in March 2006. In June of that year his mother, Tracey Connelly, began a relationship with a new boyfriend, Steven Barker, who moved in to live with Tracey and her son in November. Violence towards Peter began soon afterwards and in December 2006 his mother, Tracey, was arrested after bruises were spotted on the boy's face and chest by a GP. From that moment onwards he was on the Haringey child protection register: social workers were now keeping him under surveillance. In January of the following year Peter was placed in the care of a family friend but returned home after five weeks. A month later, a former social worker, Nevres Kemal, wrote, through her lawyer, to the central government – Department of Health – to voice concerns about alleged failings in child protection in Haringey (Maier 2008). In March the Commission for Social Care Inspection (CSCI) inspectors met Haringey officials to discuss concerns raised by Kemal's letter (Ofsted 2007). (In April Ofsted took over responsibility for inspecting children's services from CSCI.) Meanwhile the following month Peter was admitted to North Middlesex hospital with bruises, two black eyes and swelling on the left side of his head.

His outward signs of abuse were becoming clear. In May, after seeing marks on the boy's face, a social worker sent Peter to the North Middlesex where 12 areas of bruises and scratches were found. This led to the subsequent re-arrest of Tracey Connelly. Meanwhile in June, Barker, her boyfriend, moved his brother, Jason Owen, into the home. Owen was accompanied by a 15-year-old girl.

Yet the abuse continued and Connelly and Barker took steps to hide it from view. At the end of July, injuries to Peter's face and hands were missed by a social worker after the boy was deliberately smeared with chocolate to hide them. At the beginning of August, at the insistence of social workers, the boy was examined at a child development clinic. Meanwhile the outcome of Tracey Connelly's arrest in May was that the Crown Prosecution Service decided not to proceed further with the case and the police informed her of this. It was the following day, 3rd August 2007, that Peter was found dead in his cot.

In the subsequent trial in November 2008, Owen and Barker were found guilty of causing the death of Baby Peter. Tracey Connelly had pleaded guilty to the same charge and sentence was delayed 'for legal reasons' until 22nd May 2009. At the beginning of that month Barker was convicted of raping a two-year-old girl in north London, a crime which had come to light after his arrest in connection with Baby Peter's death. In the sentence at the end of the month Tracey Connelly received an indefinite jail term with a minimum term of five years for her part in her son's death. Barker was jailed for life with a minimum of ten years for raping the two-year-old and given a 12-year term to run concurrently for his role in Baby Peter's death. Owen received an indefinite sentence with a minimum term of three years (Department of Education 2010a, 2010b).

As with London Probation, what made matters worse at Haringey was that this was the same borough in which the same thing had happened a few years previously. In 2000 eight-year-old Victoria Climbié was murdered following extreme abuse and neglect (Laming 2003). She had died under the noses of police, social services of not only Haringey but three other local authorities, the Health Service and the National Society for the Prevention of Cruelty to Children (NSPCC), all of whom had noted signs of abuse but had failed to investigate the case properly. This fact alone inevitably meant a high media profile for the Baby Peter case.

A system in crisis?

When a murder takes place it is a tragedy for the victim, their relatives and friends. The public at large will feel a mixture of sympathy for the victims and, especially in the case of a seemingly random killing like those committed by Sonnex and Farmer, a concern that similar things could conceivably strike other people they know or even themselves.

There will inevitably be criticism of the authorities and the criticism of the probation service or child protection social work will be particularly severe in cases like those outlined above. The police also earn periodic criticism for low clear up rates for crime in general or for failure to solve a particular high profile case but the police are predominantly a proactive agency tracking the perpetrators of crimes already committed. They will earn public praise for an early arrest and maybe public apprehension and criticism for a long drawn out inconclusive investigation. They are however less likely to be criticised for allowing a crime to take place under their very noses. The courts periodically come in for criticism about the laxity of sentencing and the failure to hand down sentences regarded as sufficiently punitive or capable of deterring other potential offenders. In particular cases where the public, or the media at least, see a sentence as derisory, a judge may be pilloried for a time in the popular press.

But when murder occurs by someone already known to, and under the legal surveillance of, probation officers or when a vulnerable child already under the supervision of child protection social workers becomes a victim at the hands, not of strangers but of family members already known to those same social workers, then the sense of tragedy and frustration will be all the more acute because the murder will be seen to have been preventable. It is not a question of tracking down a killer or taking adequate preventative measures or inflicting adequate punishment: the offender was already under our control or the potential victim was already in our safekeeping and those most likely to inflict injury or death were already known to us. Protection is what probation officers and child protection social workers do! The criticism will be that much stronger because of the feeling that the crime ought to have been preventable if everyone concerned was doing their job properly. Why didn't the social workers or probation officers notice what was going on and why didn't they do anything about it? These are the questions immediately asked – by individuals, victims' relatives, the local community where the crime takes place and the general public. The media may have a field day particularly if, as in the case of both Sonnex and Baby Peter, the incident can be seen as linking in with general public anxieties about violent crime and the safety of vulnerable children. There is immediate demand for accountability, a strong temptation to find someone to blame, both managers and front line practitioners: and to the extent that real negligence can be established this is of course appropriate even if the tenor of media representation leaves much to be desired.

When the media and public furore, if there is one, has died down, those responsible for picking up the pieces – which generally means those working in or directly associated with probation or social services – need to concern themselves with three issues. First, there is a need to get a sense of proportion. What situation is society actually facing? Were these events 'one off' failures or are they a symptom that the system in general is coping less and less with the problems it is supposed to deal with? Is it on the verge of some sort of crisis?

This connects with a second issue: can a recurrence be prevented? Are we dealing with the fact of human error that will inevitably occur from time to time even in the most efficient organisations or are there some changes that can be made to reduce the likelihood of recurrence? If so what types of changes? In particular how much mileage is there to be gained from refining and tweaking existing methods of working or, by contrast, have fundamental flaws in working methods been revealed such that only a wide ranging rethink will make any difference? As we shall see, such issues are at the moment under active debate in both probation and social work.

There is also and importantly a third issue which gets some discussion within the social work and probation agencies but which is very easy to leave in the background or gloss over because it seems less possible to do anything about it in the immediate sense at least within the day-to-day working of the agencies. This issue concerns the general social and political environment within which the agencies work and the impact of broad social and political changes on the working of agencies like social work and probation. How far, for example, have changes in the nature of community life, the structure of the family or the forms of employment made more difficult the tasks of these agencies? Politically, have changes in political ideology such as increased emphasis on punitiveness or the prioritisation of public protection affected the work of the agencies and in what ways? Have expectations, for example, been raised by politicians to absurdly high levels in terms of the protection of the public from violent crime or child abuse such that when – mercifully rare – failures occur the public, media and political reactions tend to be increasingly severe?

The 1970s and today

These and similar questions are the subject matter of this book and different aspects of them will be taken up in the chapters that follow. However, it should be clear that the discussion, let alone any definitive answer, requires something in the way of a historical perspective. If we want to answer the question of whether the situation is getting better or worse regarding the recurrence of the types of incidents in probation or child protection under discussion here we need to establish a time period over which we can look at changes. The same applies to questions of working methods and in particular to issues of social and political change. We need to establish a time period over which we can establish the patterns of change.

For this reason I have selected the 1970s as a comparison period. Not only does 40 years seem a period long enough to detect shifts and changes but also this was a period during which an iconic case of death by child neglect and abuse, the case of Maria Colwell, occurred in 1973. Comparisons between the present situation regarding Baby

Peter and Victoria Climbié and that of Maria Colwell are frequently made (see for example Parton 1985, 2004) and will be an important theme in this book. From the standpoint of probation it is difficult to find any case that achieved such importance as the tragedy of Maria Colwell but there is the less well known case of Graham Young who committed his bizarre crimes of poisoning while under probation supervision in 1971. The Young and Colwell cases will serve as two comparison points to anchor the discussion about a number of important changes. The main details of each case can be briefly summarised.

Maria Colwell was born in 1965 in Hove and was seven years old when she died on 6th January 1973. Maria was one of nine children but had spent five years in the foster care of her aunt, finally being returned to her mother Pauline at the age of six-years and eight-months to live in Brighton. By this time her mother was no longer living with Maria's father and had a new partner, William Kepple. Kepple had children of his own and tended to favour them at the expense of Maria; for example he would buy them ice creams and force Maria to watch while they ate them. Despite reports from neighbours and teachers of concerns about ill-treatment and her appearance as a 'walking skeleton', Maria was allowed to remain in this situation with her step-siblings. Finally, on the night of 6th January 1973 she was taken to the Royal Sussex County Hospital in Brighton with injuries including brain damage and she died shortly after arrival. She had been starved and beaten to death by her stepfather. William Kepple was convicted of manslaughter and sentenced to eight years in prison but had his sentence halved on appeal (Field-Fisher 1974).

Maria had been placed on a supervision order to the local authority from the time of her return to her mother and during the time Maria lived with her mother and stepfather she was visited by a variety of social workers. In the months preceding her death there were 50 official visits to her home – from the NSPCC, the police, school welfare officers, housing officials, social workers and health visitors. None of these agencies however saw the complete picture. She stopped attending school in November 1972 and ran away from home several times and there was general concern about her care expressed by a schoolteacher and by numerous neighbours to the NSPCC. Maria was part of an extended family well known on the estate where they lived.

However despite these concerns being reported, Maria was battered to death by her stepfather on the night of 5/6 January 1973. At the time of her death she was found to weigh only three quarters of what would be expected for a child of her age and height. Kepple had a poor physical health record and had been convicted previously for relatively minor offences of violence on two occasions. A Department of Health and Social Security (DHSS) report was published in September 1974 concerning Maria Colwell's death (Parton 1985).

Graham Young was born in North London in 1947. The first two years of his life were spent with his aunt Winnie and her husband, Jack, and Graham became very close to them. In 1950 his father remarried reunited the family in St. Albans with his new wife, Molly. Graham showed visible signs of distress at being separated from his aunt (Bowden 1996).

From a young age he developed a fascination for poisons and in 1961 at the age of 14 he started to test poisons on his family, making them violently ill. In 1962 his young stepmother Molly died from poisoning. Young's aunt Winnie became suspicious knowing that her nephew was fascinated by poisons and seeing that the other members of the family – his father and sister – as well as a school friend were suffering nausea and sickness.

Young was eventually sentenced to 15 years in Broadmoor mental hospital, an institution for mentally unstable criminal offenders. He served nine years and was seen as fully recovered although it later transpired he had been studying poisons during the whole period of the sentence (Aarvold et al. 1973). In 1971 Young was released from hospital and sent to a rehabilitation centre. He then began work as a storekeeper at a factory which manufactured the chemical thallium for military use. The factory was at Bovingdon and near his sister's home in Hemel Hempstead. Within two months of his release he was buying dangerous poisons again.

No one who dealt with him was informed of his background or his previous history, not even the probation officer whom he was told to visit every two weeks. The director of Broadmoor said that if they thought there had been any risk at all of his re-offending they would not have released him in the first place. Although he was being supervised by a probation officer on his release from Broadmoor, Young's employers were never informed of his previous convictions.

This was not an oversight but was seen as a key part of his rehabilitation programme. His employers knew that he had had 'mental problems' that accounted for his lack of an employment history but they took the laudably unprejudiced view that everyone deserved a chance and that no one's past should be held against him. His probation officer never visited either his home or his workplace (Aarvold et al. 1973).

Soon after he began work at the factory Bob Elge, a foreman, became ill and subsequently died. Among Young's responsibilities was making tea for his colleagues and, unsurprisingly in retrospect, a sickness spread through the workplace which was mistaken for a virus and nicknamed the Bovingdon Bug. Over the next few months Young poisoned 70 people and he was discovered when another work colleague, Fred Biggs, became ill and died after having been admitted to the London National Hospital for Nervous Diseases. Young made hints to the company doctor and colleagues that he was interested in poisons and that thallium poisoning could be the cause of his colleagues deaths. Young was arrested on 21st November 1971 when police discovered poisons and a detailed diary in his flat where he recorded the doses he had administered to his colleagues. Young pleaded guilty at St. Albans Crown Court and was sentenced to life imprisonment. He died at the age of 42 in Parkhurst prison in 1990.

The Graham Young case attracted considerable publicity due to the nature of his crime. A film entitled 'The Young Poisoner's Handbook' was produced in 1995 (Ross 1995) and there continues to be fascination with Young's crimes, to such a degree that in November 2005 a 16-year-old Japanese schoolgirl tried to re-enact the poisoning of her mother with thallium having become fascinated by Young after seeing the film (Lewis 2005). For this discussion what is most interesting about this case is something else: the lack of any focus on the role of the probation service in Young's supervision. As we have mentioned, the probation officer concerned with Young seems to have made little attempt to discover much about him or communicate with his family and post-release employers. The only focus on those who supervised him seems to have been the criticism of Broadmoor hospital.

Equipped with these anchor points I, before concluding this introduction, turn briefly to the first of our themes – the extent of the problem and how it has developed over time.

As regards child abuse related deaths it is fortunate I am able to refer to the recent statistical work of Colin Pritchard and Richard Williams (2010) who, in an exhaustive statistical study from the time of Maria Colwell to the present, were able to show that in England child abuse related deaths for children up to age 14 in terms of absolute numbers fell from 1,762 in 1974–6 to 549 in 2004–6, a decline of 69 percent (Pritchard & Williams 2010: 1709). In terms of rate per million children this was a fall from 223 in 1974–6 to 54 in 2004–6, a fall of 67 percent (Pritchard & Williams 2010: 1712). While, as they note, it is not possible to isolate the effect of child protection measures from more general factors such as demography, public health and economic development, the fact that the fall in England and Wales was one of the sharpest in the developed world indicates that improved child protection measures probably played a considerable role. The Baby Peter and Victoria Climbié cases occurred, in other words, against a background of general improvement over the 30 years since Maria Colwell.

Historical trends regarding offenders who commit serious further offences (SFOs) while under probation supervision are not possible to plot at the present time. At the time of Graham Young's murders figures on what would now be called SFOs are difficult to come by. Thus a study of a hundred probation 'failures' in the early 1970s (Hesketh & Hewitt 1972) began without any attempt to produce accurate statistics by simply referring to the fact that the substantial amount of unrecorded crime must include a considerable amount committed by those under probation supervision:

> At December 31, 1970, there were some 84,969 probation orders in force in England and Wales, and in the year 1970 some 855,387 unsolved indictable offences. Many probationers are sufficiently involved in criminal activity to make one suspect that if the police "success" rates went up, the probation "success" rates would go down (Hesketh & Hewitt 1972: 391).

It is interesting that such a vague association is allowed to pass but this is perhaps an indication of the extent to which the issue was not really prioritised at the time. So comparison with the earlier period along the lines of the data on child protection does not seem to be possible. What can be said, however, is that at the time of the

Sonnex murders, when the media moral panic (see Chapter 2) was in full swing, the occurrence of similar events as a proportion of the total probation caseload was very small and it has shown no tendency to rise in recent years. Although around the time of Sonnex the recording practices were being changed, for the few years up to that point the Offender Case Management Statistics issued by the Ministry of Justice (Ministry of Justice 2009) give some indication of absolute numbers of SFOs involving murder or manslaughter:

> During 2007–8, 1300 cases of serious further offending by offenders under the supervision of the Probation Service were subject to review following notification to NOMS (National Offender Management Service) Public Protection Unit. Of these cases (as at 15th May 2009), 672 offenders were convicted of a serious further offence (SFO) and 230 offenders were convicted of a less serious offence. 300 cases did not result in a conviction, and 60 cases are still to be concluded.
>
> Of these 672 SFOs 106 involved cases of murder, attempted murder or manslaughter.
>
> During 2008–9, 1,100 cases of serious further offending by offenders under the supervision of the Probation Service were subject to review following notification to NOMS Public Protection Unit. Of these cases (as at 11th May 2009), 360 offenders were convicted of an SFO and 130 offenders were convicted of a less serious offence. 150 cases did not result in a conviction; and 430 cases are still to be concluded.
>
> Of these 362 SFOs 45 involved cases of murder, attempted murder or manslaughter.
>
> (Ministry of Justice 2009: 42–6).

Thus in terms of a national probation caseload of 178,115 in 2007 and 176,220 in 2008, these SFO convictions as a whole amount to 0.37 percent in 2007 and 0.2 percent 2008 while the murder, attempted murder and manslaughter cases involved even fewer. These figures for convictions obviously exclude SFOs for which the offender had yet to be convicted in the courts.

For London, where both the Sonnex and the Hanson and White cases occurred, the supervision caseload made up of offenders on community orders and licence (i.e. sentenced to community punishment or released from custody on licence excluding those still in custody but under probation supervision) in 2006 was 20,000 and remained fairly static around 25,000 up to 2009 (London Probation Board 2009: 22). Of this total caseload those charged (not necessarily convicted) of all categories of SFOs (murder, attempted murder, manslaughter, rape, arson with intent to endanger life, kidnapping/ abduction, other serious violent or sexual offences) amounted in 2006 to 0.5 percent (Ansbro 2006: 58). It is clear therefore that these phenomena have a low incidence (and in the case of child abuse related deaths definitely falling in the long run) but also have a high public profile.

The second set of issues surround the question of how to minimise recurrence. It cannot be stressed too much that where murder and manslaughter are concerned it is not enough to point out that the proportion of killings of children under social services protection or by offenders on probation licence is small. A death is a tragedy and all available strategies for preventing recurrence must be given serious consideration.

The issues here concern what lessons can be learned from the tragedies that do occur. What reforms need to be made, procedures changed, resources increased? This is generally the work of internal inquiries which, depending on the preceding media and public profile of the incident, may themselves, like the inquiry chaired by Lord Laming into the death of Victoria Climbié and his re-engagement for a further inquiry into child protection in general following the death of Baby Peter, assume a degree of publicity. Others, like those conducted in London Probation after the Sonnex murders, may be more low profile and in-house although, as we shall see later (in Chapters 4 and 5), the two sets of inquiries have much in common in terms of methodology.

It is at this stage that some of the key questions emerge: is it a question of tightening or further 'tweaking' of existing procedures and approaches? The comparative rarity of the events may suggest this is the correct orientation and this has been the dominant approach. On the other hand it is not beyond the bounds of possibility that the low rate of incidents is more due to the hard work and dedication of practitioners working 'outside' the formal procedures than it is something which flows from the procedures which, formally at least, govern their actions. Indeed it is entirely possible that the sources of failure can be located in those very formal procedures themselves and hence similar failures may be more likely in the future if working methods are not changed. This issue, as illustrated in Chapter 5, constitutes the basis of a wider debate that has increasing prominence in both probation and child protection.

Interactions

Thirdly, there are the wider issues of social and political change and the extent to which these have hindered or assisted the work of probation and child protection. The focus for a discussion of these factors will be changes in the orientation of central government towards failures by social services or probation. Here the historical comparison will be important. The fact that the dismissal of Sharon Shoesmith from Haringey Children's Services or the 'assisted resignation' of David Scott from London Probation have no parallel at the time of Maria Colwell and Graham Young and that the behaviour of senior government ministers was entirely different will enable us to see some of the changes in British politics over the intervening 30 years and how they have impacted on the work of probation and child protection. This will be the subject of Chapter 4. It will be preceded first by a discussion of the role of the media (Chapter 2) in which the contrast with the earlier period in terms of moral panic and the media pillorying of both front line practitioners and senior managers, particularly in the Baby Peter case, will be drawn out. This will then facilitate the discussion in Chapter 4 of how the relation between government and mass media has been a key component of the changing response of ministers to Sonnex and Baby Peter as compared with Colwell and Young.

Chapter 3 will be devoted to a discussion of the changing role of community over the period between the two pairs of incidents and its impact both on the work of child protection and probation and on the role of the media and politics. While each chapter will focus on a particular theme – Chapter 2 on the media, Chapter 3 on the community, Chapter 4 on government and Chapter 5 on the debate about methods of work – the key themes of media, government, community and agency working methods will (hopefully) be in continuous interaction.

In Chapter 6 I shall conclude with a survey of some of the new, and not so new, themes which have emerged following the emergence of the coalition government following the election of May 2010 and attempt to identify some of the contradictions in policy and the likely outcomes.

In criminology it was the Left Realist school that taught us to see crime control as essentially a dynamic interactive process involving a number of different types of actors. Left Realism attempted to portray the importance of these interactions in terms of a 'Square of Crime' (Lea 1992; Young 1987, 1992; see also Lea 2002) specified as the interaction between four components of law enforcement, the wider community and public, the victim and the offender.

I attempt to use a similar methodology in this book seeing the four components of media, government, community and agency (i.e. child protection and probation) as forming a square of interacting parts. It is to be hoped that by using this framework of interaction the various themes developed by several scholars and practitioners who have studied both probation and social work and the environments in which they currently operate can be brought into fruitful relation.

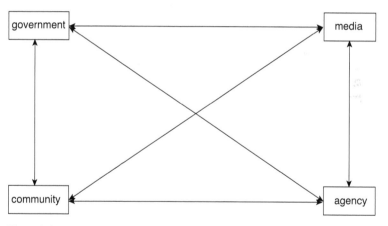

Figure 1.1 Interactions

Finally, in all the chapters a key element I have tried to keep in focus is how the situation looks to the practitioner: what practitioners feel has gone wrong and needs to be put right. To this end I benefited from the substantial interviews I was able to conduct, during 2009–10 with several managers and front line practitioners both in probation and social work. I was fortunate in being able to interview five probation managers and six probation officers working in public protection and two social work managers and three social work practitioners all of whom had experience in child protection. I am indebted to them for the time they gave up to talk to me and it is my hope that I have been able to reflect at least some of their concerns and hopes for the future in the pages of this book.

2
Media Responses

Tragic events such as the death of a child through violence and neglect or a particularly brutal murder naturally attract the attention of the print and broadcast media. In a democracy the public has a right to know about such events. There may be frictions between media inquiry and other responses such as police or official investigations. There may also be frictions between journalists and the right to everyday privacy of relatives of the victims or practitioners from the criminal justice and other agencies involved in the cases. Interests conflict but nevertheless it is fundamental to an open society that the media has a right to investigate the facts, form opinions and broadcast its conclusions.

However media coverage is never simply informative. Generations of social scientists have attempted to assess the role of the mass media in influencing and shaping public opinion rather than simply investigating 'facts' and reflecting the opinions that various sections of the public already have (Chibnall 1977; Cohen & Young 1981; Critcher 2009; Greer 2011). As we shall see, concepts like 'media moral panic' are particularly relevant in the cases studied here and indeed illustrate the problems of all research which both relies on the media as a source of information about what happened and at the same time sees media portrayal as one component of the events being investigated (see Peelo 2006). This study is no exception. The aim in this chapter is to establish a critical perspective on the media portrayal of the events under consideration but at the same time in this and the other chapters newspapers and other media have to be relied upon as sources of information on those same events. It is difficult to separate these out because what we want to understand is the changing of public attitudes from the Colwell/Young to the Baby Peter/Sonnex events. Those attitudes are reflected in the media and part of the change which is my focus is itself a changed relationship between the public and the media and indeed, as shall be argued later, the media and politics and the relative capacity of each as opinion formers.

A final point is that in looking at media coverage the focus is mainly on newspapers which might seem a somewhat outdated approach in the age of 24 hour broadcast and internet. Nevertheless in terms of media influence, as opposed to simply opinion and information, the print media is probably still dominant and its various 'feature' and 'opinion' sections more able to develop arguments than the tighter format of television news for example (Altheide 2009: 81).

Child deaths: Offenders and victims

There was plenty of national press reporting of the Maria Colwell inquiry and as Parton (1985) observes it was the inquiry rather than the death of Maria itself which became the focus of national media attention. The only coverage of Colwell's death by the national press at the time of the case was the appeal court verdict halving the sentence of her stepfather William Kepple to four years for manslaughter, the rest of the coverage occurred during the public inquiry as a result of the pressure arising directly from the local residents. There are a number of complex dynamics at work which make the media treatment of the Maria Colwell case very different from that of Baby Peter.

The national press – the *Mirror, Sun, Daily Mail and News of the World* as well as broadsheets such as *The Guardian* – all gave considerable coverage at the stage of the inquiry. There was condemnation, particularly of Maria's stepfather William Kepple who had been prosecuted for her murder. He was frequently characterised as a 'brute' (see e.g. 'Brute moved to new jail', *Sunday Mirror*, 28th October 1973) and in this respect the attitude of the press was not dissimilar to that in the case of Steven Barker, the boyfriend of Tracey Connelly who was convicted of the murder of her son Baby Peter.

However, Maria's mother, Pauline Kepple, found some sympathy in the national press, in contrast to Tracey Connelly, the mother of

Baby Peter, 30 years later. The *News of the World* said that 'any woman who has ever had to cope – alone – with a maniacal drunkard will know that there was very little Mrs. Kepple could have done' (*News of the World*, 22nd April 1973 'What could Mrs. Kepple do?', quoted in Butler & Drakeford 2008: 376). Later that year *The Guardian* claimed that Maria's mother 'has been through the most terrible time emotionally and in her social and economic conditions' and continued:

> There is a breaking point of a mother. In this case, a woman who has been through all these experiences and is in an emotional state is being asked to do a job which is beyond her. She was not able to manage her family successfully under these conditions (*Guardian* Reporter 1973a).

In December 1973 as the inquiry drew to a close national press reporting contained a good deal of sympathy for Pauline Kepple and her having to put up with, and trying to defend Maria from, her violent partner. There was, however, doubt about the truth of many of Pauline Kepple's statements to the inquiry (see Butler & Drakeford 2008: 377). Indeed, there were other dynamics that interacted with the reporting by the national press. First, the inquiry itself provided a forum in which independent local voices could be heard – witnesses, neighbours, teachers, local officials concerned with child protection – and they did not by any means echo the orientations of the national press. It is important to remember that the Inquiry set up by Sir Keith Joseph was as a result of local pressure from campaigners in Brighton and most of the reporting of the case had hitherto been restricted to the local press – in particular the Brighton *Argus*. The fact that the Inquiry was located in Sussex, near to where the tragedy had taken place, meant that local voices were heard. The actual activities and role of neighbours will be discussed in the next chapter. What is significant here is that they often produced a view of the case which diverged from that of the national press. For example a less harsh view of Maria's stepfather William Kepple and a harsher view of Maria's mother Pauline Kepple emerged from local voices at the inquiry.

In the press, he was routinely presented as a hard drinking, fiery-tempered Irish labourer, living in mainland Britain during the height of the 1970s IRA bombing campaign. Yet, the picture of Mr Kepple presented by witnesses to the public inquiry was far more ambivalent. The picture of a generally hard-working, rather anxious home-maker, rough but with a ready relationship with his own children, uneducated but very far from inarticulate, that emerges from some of the seventy oral witnesses to the inquiry is entirely absent from newspaper reporting. It also stood in sharp contrast to local accounts of Mrs Kepple's character and previous history. Witnesses reminded the inquiry that it was Mrs Kepple's failure to provide for the newly born Maria that had led to her reception into care in the first instance. It was at her insistence that Maria had subsequently been returned to her, from the paternal aunt and uncle by whom she had then been brought up for more than six years. While it was William Kepple who was prosecuted for Maria's murder, it was against Mrs Kepple that many of those neighbours who had known the family at closest quarters made complaints to the NSPCC [National Society for the Prevention of Cruelty to Children] (Drakeford & Butler 2010: 1424).

Local reporting of the case of Maria Colwell included Pauline Kepple being called a 'bloody murderess' ('Shouts at the cemetery as little Maria is buried' *Argus* 28th January 1973). Even when attending the Inquiry itself she was taunted and jostled by a group of women outside the court and called 'a witch' ('Witch taunt at Maria's Mother' *Daily Mirror* 1st November 1973). These sentiments, irrespective of their questionable moral substance, do not appear at that time to be the *result* of a national media hysteria but rather of autonomous local actions. Moral panic may have been an aspect of the Colwell case but, as Nigel Parton later commented,

It was not the death of Maria as a dramatic event in itself but the public inquiry following the decision of the secretary of state, Sir Keith Joseph, that sensitised the public and the media to the issue of child abuse (Parton 1985: 72).

I shall return to the issue of moral panic presently but meanwhile what is clear even from a cursory examination of the Maria Colwell case is that there is no monolithic media message comparable to that surrounding the death of Baby Peter over 30 years later. The positions of the national press diverge from those of the local press, the latter tending to keep close to the values of its readers (Peelo 2006). The latter is also important because until the inquiry, a response to local pressure, the incident is mainly a local issue. There are a diversity of voices and those reflected in the Inquiry are by no means coterminous with those of the national media. At the same time the inquiry itself inevitably gave an orientation to national press reporting. The inquiry was the main source of national press reports and it focused on responsibilities – whether the social worker and the NSPCC could have acted differently, the opinions of neighbours, the character of the Kepples and the wider issues of the development of a strategy against the cycle of child abuse (Parton 1985). What the inquiry did not dwell on were the minute and graphic details of the violence which culminated in Maria's death. By the time of the murder of Baby Peter things had become rather different.

One of the contrasts between the killings of Maria Colwell and Baby Peter 34 years later is the detail with which in the latter the press forensically inspected every aspect of the case. Any notion that such terrible crimes will only be made worse by continual voyeuristic public inspection and rehearsal of every detail has disappeared. The idea of respect for the dead victim seems to have been abandoned in favour of the maxim that the more gruesome the descriptions, the more papers are sold to a general public apparently salivating for graphic details.

Tracey Connelly's partner Steven Barker played a role in many ways similar to that of William Kepple 30 years earlier. Both men were abusive and violent and directly caused the fatal injuries which killed the two children but Barker is endowed with none of the ambiguities and tensions between violent drunkard and hardworking father that characterised the various representations of Kepple. He, Barker, appears as a straightforward underclass thug lacking any redeeming features. Typical was the extended portrayal in the *Daily Mail* of Barker as a 'sadistic thug who trained [Baby Peter] like a dog...a knife obsessed sadist, he wore combat gear, collected Nazi military memorabilia including helmets and daggers decorated with swastikas and was always seen with his beloved Rottweiler' (Allen & Fernandez 2008).

Neither is there much ambiguity regarding Baby Peter's mother, Tracey Connelly. Although the *Daily Mail* article does mention that she had been raised by a drug-addicted mother and had a disastrous marriage to a violent alcoholic, any potential understanding of the origins of her plight is rapidly displaced by the theme of the burden she placed on the welfare system and the 'extraordinary resources... lavished on her, with social services paying Ann Walker, a registered childminder, to look after Baby Peter four days a week' (Allen & Fernandez 2008). Meanwhile Connelly 'chain-smoked, gossiped on Internet chat sites and played online poker' (Allen & Fernandez 2008). On the internet she allegedly claimed, according to the *Mirror,* that 'becoming a mum' was the best thing that ever happened to her (Ward 2008).

The last remnants of the traditional working class community which gave at least a semblance of humanity to Pauline and William Kepple have disappeared and we are now confronted by the media with the almost sub-human feral underclass in the form of Connelly and Barker. Carole Malone, in the *News of the World,* raises the alarm in stark terms:

> And that's what we have to address now – this underclass, this group of deviants who've been allowed to take root in this country and who kill, maim and torture without guilt.
>
> These are people who have sponged off the welfare state their whole lives and who believe nothing is their responsibility, their fault or their problem.
>
> For too long we've tap-danced around these people because of political correctness. The problem was too sensitive to talk about – let alone handle. But handle it we must, because if we don't this underclass will become even more savage, more feral and more innocents will die (Malone 2008).

This familiar right-wing theme of welfare profligacy having created such a stratum is given an outing by well known *Daily Mail* columnists Melanie Phillips and Peter Hitchens. Phillips blames the 'shattered social landscape of lost and abandoned children raised in households of gross emotional chaos and physical and moral squalor' on a Leftist progressive intelligentsia which 'systematically trashed and up-ended the fundamental values of a civilized society...and caused drug abuse, crime and systematic dishonesty as a way of life' (Phillips 2008). Hitchens, meanwhile, sees clearly that the reason for the failure of social services to intervene to save Baby Peter lies in the fact that 'social workers are increasingly fearful of the violent, conscience-free underclass created by 45 years of well-intentioned but disastrous socialism' (Hitchens 2008).

The deployment of child death as a vehicle for a frontal attack on the welfare state marks a significant difference from the time of Maria Colwell when notwithstanding a moral panic about the decline of the family the consensus was still that of devising new strategies for the welfare agencies to overcome the 'cycle of deprivation' through more precise and structured forms of intervention (Parton 1985).

Yet perhaps the greatest contrast is the computer-assisted voyeurism which attended the suffering and death of Baby Peter. A description of Maria Colwell as an injured child is not absent from media accounts. Thus *The Guardian* reported 'Mrs Shirley Ruston, who lived next door to Maria in Maresfield Road told the Inquiry that she once saw the child with her face blackened by bruises and with one eye virtually a pool of blood' (Mackie 1973). Media comment however, even in the tabloids, largely keeps a respectful distance and remains content with medicalised descriptions. The trial of Kepple, at which more details of Maria's injuries might have been available to the press, remained, as we have seen, a local matter.

The *Mirror* reporting the Inquiry is even more circumspect than *The Guardian*:

In the autumn months of last year neighbours say they heard screams and saw bruises on the child. Her teacher worried about her palour and thinness, her absence from school...Maria died with terrible injuries and weighed only 36 lbs – just two thirds of a seven-year-old's average weight (Walker 1973).

In the case of Baby Peter, the main source of detail is the trial of Barker. *The Guardian* usually maintained a neutral medical tone.

A postmortem examination revealed the boy had a broken back, eight fractured ribs, missing fingernails and toenails, multiple bruises and an injury to the inside of his mouth. He had also swallowed one of his own teeth. The court heard that his back had been broken by slamming him down over a bent knee or a bannister, which would have left him paralysed (Siddique & Jones 2008).

Less so the *Daily Mail* and the *Mirror*. Alongside the use of computer generated images of the injuries to Baby Peter there are more vivid descriptions based on the testimony of one of the prosecution witnesses, a 15-year-old teenager who lived next door to Baby Peter. The *Daily Mail* revealed details of the testimony of which a small sample will suffice:

> The 15-year-old, who was a key prosecution witness at the trial over Baby P's death...said his fingernails were pulled out with pliers and fingertips cut off during the sickening torture in the eight months before he died...He was grabbed by the throat and thrown into his cot, had his windpipe pressed so hard he turned blue and a bottle rammed into his mouth with such force that it cut his lips (*Daily Mail* Reporter 2008).

The *Mirror* reported in much the same style. While in 1973 Maria Colwell 'died with terrible injuries' the portrait of the violence to Baby Peter is graphic:

> Social worker Maria Ward visited twice a week but the hulking brute of a boyfriend always hid. She saw the boy head butting the carpet. It was later discovered that the boyfriend would click his fingers as he did for his Rottweiler dog to make the boy put his head down in fear of another beating. He tortured the toddler, squeezing his fingernails, hitting him and throwing him around the room (Clements & Shaw 2008).

Partly of course the revolution in media technology in the intervening 30 years accounts for the much more graphic descriptions of Baby Peter but, reading the accounts of Maria Colwell, one has the feeling that even if computer-simulated pictures of injuries were possible at the time it would have been regarded as too intrusive to use them. If Maria's death was a tragedy, a family gone wrong, Baby Peter's is sadistic torture in which the lurid descriptions with their macabre visual aids add up to an emotional horror movie populated by monsters and helpless victims.

This change in visual and media presentation echoes the transition in language from concern for the deprived community to fear of the feral underclass, and the transition in the status of the poor from tragedy to threat. What happened to Baby Peter could happen to others. The feckless mother and the brutal offender are exemplary of the feral underclass which threatens to drag us down to its level and against which it is the duty of the agencies to protect us. The community – as the media portrays it – does not itself display any feeling of responsibility. Responsibility is entirely placed on the agencies who should, and could, have prevented it happening. This, as we shall see in the next chapter, contrasts with the Colwell case. Today, the greater sense of public isolation and the fragmentation of communities has increased both public fears and paranoia about such violent offences occurring and stimulated a fascination with their details. This in turn has fuelled the media reaction. The impulse to deploy graphic intrusion amounting to voyeurism is a profound reflection of the fear which these events engendered – even if the media did exaggerate it. Moral panic has become a normalised reaction to events such as the death of Baby Peter and the murders by Dano Sonnex.

Murder on licence

The similarities between the murders committed by Graham Young and Dano Sonnex are mainly from the practitioner end. Both are cases of murders by individuals while under the supervision of the probation service but as crimes they are very different. Sonnex (and Farmer's) orgy of drug-fuelled violence contrasts with the calm, calculated actions of Young spread over a period. If Young has a more recent analogy it is probably the poisoning by drug overdose of up to 350 of his patients by the GP Harold Shipman for which he received 15 consecutive life sentences.

However, even here there is a crucial difference. Shipman was completely ordinary. Yvonne Jewkes (2004) asks why it was that Shipman, the most prolific serial killer in British history, avoided vilification in the media. She concludes that:

> Crimes like those of Dr. Shipman do not become the stuff of media sensation precisely because the constitutive features of the case (a middle-class professional male perpetrator; elderly, mostly

female victims; non-violent means of death) cannot be consigned to the unknown and unknowable margins. They invite society to recognise that it is not simply 'evil' or 'mad' people who are capable of killing, and this is an unpalatable truth that society is simply not ready to contemplate (Jewkes 2004: 202).

Shipman is at the other end of the spectrum from Barker and Sonnex and their associates, the demons who have come to symbolise the fears and insecurities of modern life. Young is somewhere in the middle. On the one hand he appears as 'ordinary' and his chosen means of killing lacked the graphic violence of the death of Baby Peter or, as we shall see, Sonnex's crazed orgy of bloodletting but on the other hand he was already a killer, on parole licence from Broadmoor secure mental hospital where he had been sent on a 15 year sentence for poisoning members of his family. Furthermore the death of his victims could less easily than with Shipman's elderly patients, be put down to 'natural causes'. The local press is the most graphic:

> Mr Batt lived at Harlow, and he and Young worked late in the stores to miss the traffic on the way home, said Mr Hayden. 'Mr Batt would drop Young off at his digs in Maynard Road, Hemel Hempstead.' It was on one such occasion Mr Batt had drank the 'bitter' coffee. Both Mr Batt and another man had lost all their hair by the time they were discharged from hospital, the latter having lost over a stone and described by the consultant as looking like 'a three-quarters plucked chicken'.
>
> In November, Fred Biggs, fell ill again with the 'bug', after drinking tea. He was taken to hospital in Hemel Hempstead, where his skin began to peel off. He was examined by seven doctors before being transferred to the National Hospital for Nervous Diseases, London, where he died. The feeling, among staff, was that the 'bug' was down to either water contamination, or radio-active contamination from the nearby former Bovingdon airfield, but the factory premises were examined by the Medical Officer of Health who found nothing wrong (*Watford Observer* 1972).

As far as the national press is concerned, alongside similar accounts of his unfortunate victims, the over-riding concern was the question of how on earth the modern state, with an army of doctors, psychiatrists, police and probation officers, could have allowed this man to repeat exactly the crimes for which he had been sentenced to a secure mental institution. We are horrified but don't imagine for one moment it would happen to us or that there is anything in particular we could have done to prevent the crime. In this sense Young was anything but 'ordinary' and the authorities should have known this and acted accordingly.

With the recent murders by Dano Sonnex and his accomplice Nigel Farmer we are back to the graphic descriptions of violence of the type which only nine months previously had been inflicted on Baby Peter and the media treatment of Sonnex has a similar character to that of Baby Peter. As with the description of the injuries inflicted on Baby Peter, the press left little to the imagination regarding the violence and ferocity of Sonnex and Farmer's frenzied attack on the French students Laurent Bonomo and Gabriel Ferez. This from *The Mirror* reporting on the court trial is typical:

In June last year, the two students, dressed only in their underpants, were woken in the night and tied up after Sonnex and Farmer climbed through an open window.

They stripped, hooded and tied up their victims before repeatedly beating and stabbing them for their bank cards and pin numbers in a three-hour 'orgy of bloodletting'.

Fuelled by drink and drugs, the robbers egged each other on to an "inhuman" attack of "brutal and sustained ferocity", the Old Bailey heard.

After torturing the students, Sonnex went to a cash machine (below) to withdraw money while Farmer ransacked the flat and seized Playstations and mobile phones they could sell later.

Sonnex withdrew £365 from Mr Bonomo's account but when the machine swallowed Mr Ferez's card the killers took their revenge by stabbing their victims over and over again.

They were stabbed with such ferocity that four stab wounds penetrated the full thickness of Mr Bonomo's skull.

Mr Bonomo – who Farmer later said "just wouldn't die" – was stabbed 194 times and Mr Ferez suffered 50 knife wounds, some of them after his death.

Realising they had left evidence behind, Farmer returned later to set fire to the flat but was engulfed by a fireball which burned his face and hands (Wood & Lynch 2009).

It should be emphasised that the murders were truly an orgy of violence and that the terminology in quotes is that of the prosecuting counsel and the trial judge rather than simply the imagination of the journalists. Nevertheless the assumption of the media was that the public really needed to know the details, right down to a graphic illustration of the 'horror flat' where the murders took place with outlines of where the bodies were found. From another perspective the fact that 'four stab wounds penetrated the full thickness of Mr Bonomo's skull' need not, out of respect to the victims and their families, have been broadcast to the nation.

There is however sympathy for the victims and, although they were strangers, what happened to them could happen to anyone. As with the mother and her lover in the Baby Peter case, Sonnex is the very embodiment of the feral underclass: a beast who could have unleashed his irrational orgy of violence upon any one of us. Yet, again as with Baby Peter, there is no feeling of community responsibility. There is absolutely nothing that we could have done to prevent this: rather we should have been protected and those who were supposed to protect us failed abysmally. The morbid fascination of the media with the details of the killing is both a reflection of fear and isolation and also ammunition for the widespread critique of the authorities. The Sonnex murders reinforced the furore already building up around the social workers and their managers who had allegedly failed to prevent the murder of Baby Peter.

Social work and probation on trial

With Sonnex and with any high profile case now you've got the media knocking on the door. They want to know what probation or any other agency has done wrong and whether there is any indication that we've done something wrong or not...looking who to blame, who's responsible for this and of course the reality is that the responsibility is with the offender...and sometimes that looks as if it's being forgotten and certainly Baby P. is an example where, because of the fact that there was an ongoing court case and the need to protect individuals, names weren't in the public domain and so who do you blame? You can't talk about the offender so you blame the practitioners and the managers of the practitioners. That feels very real. *Philip (Senior Probation manager)*

There was a lot of coverage of Maria Colwell and various other killings over the years particularly those from mental health units. But it didn't seem to have the same force as it does now. Partly that's because we've raised expectations. Organizations and individuals are now expected to be accountable. It's a much more politically driven structure now. They have created expectations, that all and sundry can have their say. Certainly when you look at cases from special hospitals, and prisons and mental health cases the reporting makes icons or devils or demons out of these people. There is a lot of demonizing within the media, stretching from the perpetrators of the events to the people that should have been preventing those events. That bothers me we've moved away from who commits the offence, who is accountable for the act, to the person who is managing them. There is a dual blame. The move towards blaming the system, the focus changes completely away from the perpetrator. *Morgan (Probation Manager)*

I think serious cases worsened the situation. I think it affects people's morale. At times when there's high media coverage all you ever read is negative crap about social workers not doing their job. They don't have a focus on the hard work and the positive side. It makes people more anxious about doing the work and there's a whole back covering that goes on and impacts on people. With no positives – it puts people under enormous pressure. They feel they have even more to do. It can affect individuals and teams now. After the whole Baby P. stuff there was a lot of anxiety in my team. You worry about the cases that haven't yet reached the child protection threshold or cases that are not getting the amount of attention they should be getting because there's a whole lot of other things taking priority. *Beth (Social worker)*

The reality is the press itself and the media and the way it sells its papers is good news doesn't sell and bad news does. They picked up and whipped up a frenzy that was for a period, when there was a paedophile lurking behind every bush and behind every playground. Their new target is child death and they've been able to focus their attention on what they see as failing social services and really pinpointing social services rather than other practitioners working on these cases. *Pippa – Social Work Manager*

Maria Colwell and Baby Peter

Media interest in the failures of social work began with the Maria Colwell case (Franklin & Parton 1991). There was considerable criticism of Diana Lees, the social worker responsible for Maria Colwell, and, despite the attempt of the social services director of East Sussex, Dennis Allen, to shoulder the blame, the focus at the Inquiry remained on the front line practitioner. Also the structure of social work agencies at the time meant that many of the reports by neighbours about Maria went to the NSPCC rather than directly to social services. The criticism by the Inquiry of this marked, as we shall see, the beginning of the theme of lack of co-ordination between agencies which has become a major theme in criticism of both social work and probation when things go wrong.

Nevertheless by comparison with the later cases the media gave a relatively sympathetic – or at least non-judgemental – hearing to the social workers. The vilification of Diana Lees (see next chapter) cannot with any plausibility be laid at the door of a national media campaign. Thus the *Mirror* referred to the 'Dilemma of the social workers' (3rd November 1973) and reported sympathetically the argument of senior social workers to the inquiry concerning the lack of information upon which a judgement to take Maria into care could have been made. The *Mirror* stated simply that 'an error of judgement by overstretched social workers may have cost Maria her life' (3rd November 1973).

A similar understanding is found at greater length in *The Guardian*:

Maria's death was not the fault of an individual. It was the fault of a system which set up schools and social service departments with inadequate resources. No one should sit back and say that the system had worked because in the case of Maria it had not. Mr. Peter Webster QC, for East Sussex County Council said the social workers responsible for Maria gave her care both in quality and quantity. The inquiry should avoid the trap of making some body of people scapegoats for the tragedy, he added. It was a very natural social reaction for the public to say this sort of tragedy should not occur (*Guardian* Reporter 1973b).

At the end of the day however, whatever the failures, it is the social workers and their managers who are going to sort out the issue. They are still the experts and we have to trust them and their expertise to do this. The minister responsible, Sir Keith Joseph, rather than denouncing incompetence and sacking senior social work managers was engaging in innovative thinking about how to prevent child abuse. His contribution, as is well known, was the notion of 'transmitted deprivation'. He is given a relatively sympathetic hearing by the media being interviewed by Marjorie Proops in the *Mirror* who listens with interest:

> He talked to me about the work he has instituted on a subject in which he is passionately involved: the phenomenon of transmitted deprivation.
>
> In layman's language he calls it the 'cycle of deprivation'. It means that each generation of deprived families tends to produce yet more deprived families; the problems therefore multiply at an alarming rate with each new generation.
>
> The difficulty, he says, is at what point to try to break the vicious circle (Proops 1973).

The point is not whether Joseph's approach was correct or not but that there is still at least some element of optimism that the correct application of theory to practice stands a chance of resolving social problems. By the time of Baby Peter and Dano Sonnex, although there is plenty of theory around, it is this practical optimism that has all but disappeared. It is simply a question of the agencies having failed to protect the public. The issue is to find out who is to blame and subject them to a public pillorying sufficient to shake up the organisations and prevent these things happening again. There may be some reforms in the offing but generally the invocation is to ensure better co-ordination between agencies and try and make practitioners do what they were supposed to do anyway (see Chapter 4).

More far sighted sociologists and journalists could see this coming and could identify the unfortunate symmetry in the way the public relinquish responsibility for the care and protection of the vulnerable in the community at the same time as developing a morbid and addictive fascination with the details for such cases and heaping blame on the agencies that have failed to protect. As we become more isolated and powerless and lose any feeling of responsibility towards the vulnerable outside our immediate family, so we become more fearful of, and morbidly fascinated by criminal offenders who prey on them. The sociologist Frank Furedi reflects this change in his discussion of media coverage of natural disasters such as floods.

> Until the mid-1970's, research...suggested that communities were surprisingly good at coping with even the most tragic disruptions to their lives...communities were indeed arguably able to develop modes of resilience in the face of adversity...We are dealing with...an important cultural shift...the narrative of vulnerability...that tacitly situates people and their experiences within the context of powerlessness and lack of agency (Furedi 2007: 249–250).

Meanwhile *The Guardian* journalist, Angela Neustatter, writing about Baby Peter, argued that

> as a society, we should be willing to take a good deal more responsibility for being aware of and caring of the children whose lives are lived alongside us – or, frequently, with the great divide in Britain – parallel to ours. Instead we too easily disregard "them" and concentrate only on "us".
>
> Then when an unspeakable tragedy occurs, as with Baby P, we look for those on whom we may pour our fury. Very often social workers are the ones we choose because they can all too easily be blamed for not having seen what was going on, or who are so eager to leave a child with the family they are too easily beguiled by what parents say (Neustatter 2008).

The Guardian, notwithstanding discussion of the real failures in Haringey in the Baby Peter case, generally maintained the sympathetic understanding of the problems facing social workers that it exhibited 30 years previously including staff shortages, high turnover and dangerous work. The columnist John Carvel quoted Ian Johnston, chief executive of the British Association of social workers:

> the entire press is judging us in relation to the action in one case. Social workers are not well enough supported and have to work in a culture of fear...Some of our critics would never dream of going into the situations with which we deal (Carvel 2008).

Johnston had good cause for concern. The tabloid press was frequently vitriolic in its handling of Baby Peter to the point of regarding social workers as much responsible for his death as Owen and Barker.

The *Mirror*, for example, in the first article on the trial of Owen and Barker in November 2008 mentions the failure of social workers in the same sentence as the guilt of the perpetrators:

> Two men were convicted yesterday of the death of the tortured baby after a catalogue of errors worst than in the Victoria Colombia case. The 17 month old boy suffered eight months of abuse and beatings at the hands off his mother's sadistic boyfriend. Baby Peter died despite being on the child protection register and being seen 60 times by health and social workers (Clements & Shaw 2008).

The strongest statement came from Carole Malone in the *News of the World*:

> And I'm sick to death of people saying it wasn't the social workers who killed Baby P, it was the degenerates who lived with him in that rat-infested hole. Yes, they kicked the last breath out of him...
>
> But those social workers were supposed to be better than that, professionals who were trained to spot the early signs of abuse. It was their job, their human duty to protect vulnerable children.
>
> We presumed (wrongly) that they were more intelligent than Baby P's killers, which is why we expected Maria Ward on one of the 60 times Baby P was visited to insist his mother washed chocolate off his face so she could inspect him for bruises.

And why, knowing the history, didn't she demand to check his body for injuries? She knows full well that scumbags like these killers routinely lie and cheat. But more sickening is that these social workers and executives did a better job at covering their own miserable backsides than they did at saving a little boy's life.

Which is why they ARE ultimately responsible for his death. They didn't strike the blow that killed him – but they stood by and did nothing while those three vicious bastards awaiting sentence did (Malone 2008).

The *Sun* was more activist and invited its readers to sign a petition in support of demands to sack those social workers and managers responsible.

YOU have made your voices heard in the fight for justice for Baby Peter.

In just four days, over 200,000 caring Sun readers have signed our petition to bring the people responsible for the tragic death of Baby P to justice.

We have never had such an overwhelming response to a story – but there is still more to do.

The neglect, abuse and shambolic decisions that led to the death of the 17-month-old toddler have shocked our nation. But those who could have saved him are still going unpunished.

Baby P died in his blood-soaked cot covered in bruises and paralysed from the waist down because of a broken spine.

He had been horribly abused by his mother, her boyfriend and their paedophile lodger.

The child had every chance to be saved during one of 60 visits by Haringey Social Services.

But despite Baby P being on the council's "at risk" register, the abuse went ignored. The Sun has called for the sackings of children's services boss Sharon Shoesmith, Gillie Christou who was in charge of the council's child protection register, social workers Maria Ward and Sylvia Henry and Dr Sabah Al Zayyat.

Please sign our special Sun Petition and show you care (Haydon 2008).

After the Maria Colwell case the social worker Diana Lees was spat on in the streets of Brighton. But such action was nowhere advocated in the press. It was a spontaneous (and totally inappropriate) reaction by an individual from a community that knew, and felt a degree of involvement with, Maria. The petition organised by *The Sun* illustrates the changed situation we have already noted. The only sense of collectivity and 'community' now is the virtual community of the media campaign and the sense of *virtual victimhood* which it establishes (Peelo 2006). The petition gave some people a spurious 'community involvement' in the defence of a child they did not know in a community they would never meet.

In the Colwell case there was no single media story dominated and orchestrated by the national press but a more complex interaction of local and national media, and media and community opinion. By the time of Baby Peter it is no longer a question of the relationship between the media and the community: the media *is* the community. There has been no public inquiry responding to local pressure – people are too disorganised to press for such a thing in today's fragmented communities, so local voices and attitudes of neighbours, let alone social workers, are not heard in any public forum. The subsequent inquiries have been internal and bureaucratic and concerned solely with the correct functioning of the agencies. The community is effectively annihilated while the agencies retreat behind the locked doors of internal disciplinary proceedings and at the same time receive a public flogging at the hands of the national media and their political managers.

But the tabloid hysteria did not stop at the social workers. The *bête noire* of the whole media campaign was Sharon Shoesmith the Director of Haringey Social Services. The contrast with the treatment of Dennis Allen, the Director of East Sussex Social Services at the time of the Maria Colwell case could not have been stronger. Throughout the Inquiry Allen was treated with respect as an expert and it was expected that he would be the person to draw together and implement the lessons learned from the Inquiry. It was Allen who drew the most important conclusion regarding the lack of liaison between the various agencies, in particular social services and the NSPCC, and promised to institute an internal inquiry in which the expertise of Maria's social worker, Diana Lees, would be taken into account (Cunningham 1973).

These simple lessons about agency co-ordination could well have applied to the Baby Peter case. But they were only discussed by the various subsequent reports. The Director of Social Services herself had already been dismissed by the government in the person of the Children's Secretary, Ed Balls. There was of course the added factor that Baby Peter had come so close on the heels of a very similar case, Victoria Climbié, which also occurred in Haringey. So a serious inquiry and criticism of Shoesmith and her department is entirely justified and to be expected. Indeed it may well have been that her position had become untenable. Indeed this appeared to be the position of papers like *The Guardian*. But the vitriolic personal campaign against her, together with her social workers, by sections of the tabloid media was altogether different.

Her sacking by Balls and the suspension of other social service officials after the external report into Haringey Social Services by Ofsted raised serious criticisms of the handling of Baby Peter was not enough for sections of the press. Again, probably the most vitriolic was the *News of the World*.

> Did this apology for a boss really believe that if she put on a sad face for the TV cameras she'd get away with this...and detract from her mind-boggling incompetence?
>
> Time and again she was given the chance to apologise but she didn't. Haringey council did (finally) but not Sharon Shoesmith. Because she knows an admission of guilt would require her resignation – and nothing is worth that, is it Mrs Shoesmith?
>
> Not with her cushy little number – with a £110,000 salary, posh days out at the races (paid for by grateful business contacts) and her power (Malone 2008).

Shoesmith's day at the races was taken up by the *Daily Mail*.

> Weeks after Baby P's broken body was discovered, Sharon Shoesmith could be found unwinding in luxury at Ascot.
>
> The £100,000-a-year head of children's services at Haringey enjoyed a free corporate day out with her daughter Esther.
>
> She picked five winners on the day and donated £25 of her £70 profit to a young musicians' charity in the borough.
>
> Mrs Shoesmith was at the races last year on October 13 as a guest of Willmott Dixon, one of Britain's largest privately owned construction, housing, property care and investment companies.
>
> It was ten weeks after Baby P was killed.

At the time of the junket, disturbing questions were already emerging about how an infant who suffered more than 50 injuries and visited by social workers on 60 occasions could be left to die in a bloodstained cot (Drake 2008).

If Dennis Allen went to Brighton races during the Maria Colwell inquiry – and it is not being suggested that he did – the media would probably not even have known about it. There was no concern with his image beyond that of a social services bureaucrat. By contrast the media vilification of Shoesmith resulted in an image of a heartless, hard, unfeeling and overpaid party-goer. Shoesmith appears as sinister and irresponsible.

Young and Sonnex

In probation the issue has been similar: how could probation supervision be so inadequate as to allow those under its supervision to re-offend with such terrible consequences? As with social services a key issue common to the Graham Young and Dano Sonnex cases has been that of effective communication and the passing of information between agencies. In the Maria Colwell case liaison between social services and the NSPCC was judged inadequate. In the Graham Young case, the previous year, the issue was that probation had not been informed of his history of poisoning. 'The probation service was later to complain bitterly that it was not fully informed of Graham Young's background' (Bowden 1996).

This, however, may have been due to consideration of Young's rehabilitation. Thinking in the criminal justice system at the time was still very much influenced by what David Garland (2001) calls *penal welfarism* and the idea that there was a balance between the protection of the public and the offender's right to rehabilitation. Thus the issue was cast in more complex terms than a simple failure to communicate. Young's release from Broadmoor hospital had been authorised by the then Home Secretary Reginald Maudling on the advice of the Broadmoor superintendent and psychiatrist Dr Edgar Udwin. Udwin wrote Young's reference for his job at Hadlands the photographic development company in Bovingdon. Probation officers were quite possibly therefore not informed out of a desire, misguided in this case, not to prejudice Young's chances of making a new start in rehabilitation through employment. This is not to say that his work placement in a company handling a diversity of poisonous chemicals was not a blunder of the first magnitude.

What is quite remarkable from today's perspective is that even the *Daily Express* calmly accepted this without comment:

> As Young's new trial ended in St. Albans yesterday his counsel, Sir Arthur Irvine, said 'His release from Broadmoor was a serious error of judgment with tragic consequences. The authorities had a duty to protect Young from himself as well as a duty to protect the public.'
>
> The dilemma is whether a man should be locked up forever or is safe to be given a chance to start a new life outside. As Mr Maudling put it 'A judgment must be made. Although the utmost care is taken it cannot be infallible' (Latchman et al. 1972).

What is remarkable is that by today's standards there was little in the way of a storm. No resignations, no widespread media search-light on the probation service or the competence of the Broadmoor psychiatrist and no demands for blood. Maudling made a state-ment in the House of Commons, expressed his condolences to the families of the victims and set up the inquiry under Judge Aarvold to produce recommendations for preventing similar occurrences in the future.

Today any notion of the competing claims of rehabilitation and public protection has been firmly resolved in favour of the latter. A comment in the *Daily Mail* entitled '*National shame of justice system*' set the tone for the widespread media criticism of the probation service in the Sonnex case:

> The catalogue of appalling failures that allowed a savage psycho-path like Dano Sonnex to commit two bestial murders would be disgusting enough whoever the victims were, but there is some-thing especially embarrassing for Britain that the two talented young men who were tortured to death were guests in this country...there is no question that the man who inspired the killings, Sonnex, could and should have been behind bars. British Justice failed at every level. Our Police failed to find him. Our

Prisons failed to keep him behind bars. Our magistrates failed to keep him on remand. Our Prosecutors failed by permitting his release. And above all, the probation service, whose London chief has resigned, failed to supervise him (*Daily Mail* 4th June 2009).

The fact that the families of the Sonnex's victims planned to sue the British Government gave added weight to the force of the attack launched by the media on the probation service and the government.

But what makes their sadistic torture and murder at the hands of a notorious psychopath impossible to comprehend is that it should never have happened. If the checks and protection procedures observed by any civilised country had been in place, killer Dano Sonnex would never have been out on the streets.

This psychotic beast was a ticking bomb waiting to explode. On six separate occasions probation officers, police or the courts had an opportunity to lock him up but, through sheer blundering incompetence, never did (McIntosh 2009).

The *Mail*, alongside more graphic photographs of killers and the crime scene, echoed the sentiments:

An appalling catalogue of blunders by probation officers, police and the courts allowed Dano Sonnex to rob, torture and then kill Laurent Bonomo and Gabriel Ferez.

Mr Ferez's father Olivier said an apology from Justice Secretary Jack Straw 'will not suffice' and the matter was in the hands of his lawyers.

And speaking at a press conference at Scotland Yard, Guy Bonomo said the parents knew their children 'would be alive today if the British justice system had not failed us' (Gill et al. 2009).

The *Mirror*, although scathing of the failures of probation, seems more prepared than it was in the Baby Peter case to absolve the front line practitioners from total blame:

Just one inexperienced probation officer, Susanne Blaine, was left to supervise the man who will go down in history as one of our most diabolical killers. At the time of the murders she was "drowning in paperwork" with 127 criminals on her books.

Amazing, isn't it, how often that phrase comes up. Haringey Social Services were "drowning in paperwork" when Baby P was brutally murdered.

The overworked probation officer was so buried in bureaucratic rubbish she couldn't find the time to monitor the beast who would rob, torture and kill those defenceless students in a two-hour orgy of unimaginable violence.

Not that it was her fault. She was just as much a victim of a system that has failed everyone. As the Chief Probation Officer David Scott said after his resignation over the scandal, the department is on its knees.

Every week 400 people are released from prison into the community and, as he explains, "unless this issue about workload and capacity is looked at, unless there are far more staff for probation at the frontline and unless they are supported and managed, these kind of problems will reoccur".

Wow, that inspires confidence, doesn't it? The man who knows better than anyone about the violent criminal element roaming our streets is expecting a murder like this to happen again. And again. And again. Until there is a fundamental overhaul of the criminal justice system (McIntosh 2009).

The *Mail* echoed these sentiments:

> A single newly qualified Lewisham probation officer named Suzanne Blaine, who only had a few months experience…As events would later prove, the £27,000 a year Mrs. Blaine – who had a staggering 127 criminals to monitor at the time of the murders, more than three times the usual workload – could not cope, and would go on to make a series of mistakes. A probation source said: Suzanne saw him (Sonnex) for just 20 minutes each week due to lack of time when the appointment should have been an hour (Gill et al. 2009).

There is a subtle difference in the tabloids' attitude to London probation compared with Haringey Social Services. In the latter case the social workers were guilty of negligence up to and including their Director. Probation officers made fatal mistakes but were massively overworked. Although the workload issue was not ignored in the Baby Peter case it was given less prominence and certainly did not exonerate failure.

It is clear that, in the eyes of even the tabloids, the criminal justice system has a slightly higher status than social services and probation officers are bestowed a marginally lighter touch than social workers. This is true of the head of London Area probation, David Scott, who resigned as a result of the Sonnex case. His resignation was, significantly, much more to do with the actions of the Justice Secretary Jack Straw than any media campaign (see Chapter 4). Broadsheets such as *The Guardian* remained fairly sympathetic and understanding to Scott and the probation service, while in the tabloids it is difficult to find any mention at all of his resignation. He was the mirror image of Shoesmith. While she was lifted from obscurity and portrayed by the tabloids as the arrogant, failed, uncaring parent, he never lost his status as the faceless bureaucrat known only to insiders.

To a considerable extent this is an issue of gender. Women are judged by the gendered caring role while men are accepted or constructed as ambitious, managerial and decisive. Shoesmith was a target not just because she was deviant in that she rose to a high status, managerial role, which is still unusual even in social services, but also because, psychodynamically speaking, the image of Shoesmith approached that of the 'bad mother' whose children died on her watch (Lloyd 1995; Jewkes 2004). Women who make mistakes are more likely to suffer stereotypification than men. By contrast key male figures, rarely perceived as 'bad fathers', involved in the Baby P case – male officials in Haringey council and local police chiefs – were dealt with in a more sympathetic and respectful manner.

As an extension of this the agencies themselves carry a gendered identity. The police and courts are definitely seen as 'male' and controlling while social work is traditionally seen as 'feminine' and caring. Probation used to be 'male' but has for a number of years been undergoing a transformation due to changes in pay and conditions (Annison 2007).

At another level it may well be that probation, as a criminal justice agency, was better able to handle its relations with the media than social services and indeed had responded more quickly to the Sonnex case than Haringey did with Baby Peter. One of the probation officers interviewed for this study put it in the following way:

> It seems like London probation had a better outcome than Haringey. Maybe they got what they wanted quicker in that David Scott resigned quickly. They got their scalp early on in the process. There were other drivers in that social services had just undergone large structural changes. She (Shoesmith) had come from an education background when the education and children's services merged. She hadn't been in children's services before...My guess is that there was a lot of hostility and closing down towards the media, which did not help the situation. Perhaps it was a more open approach with the criminal justice system...Also I can remember how she (Shoesmith) behaved with the press, making a very strong statement early on saying she had no responsibility for Baby P. or something like that. This wasn't the best way to manage the case. I think probation and criminal justice very early on in the Sonnex case, admitted they were to blame, saying they would look at things and learn things and I think that's got more to do with it. *Morgan – Probation Manager.*

There is one further aspect to the comparison between Baby Peter and Sonnex. With Baby Peter as far as the media were concerned incompetence and refusal to admit mistakes were personified in Sharon Shoesmith. This was reinforced by the status of social services as primarily a local authority responsibility. Ed Balls' decision to sack Shoesmith, and her subsequent unsuccessful attempts to challenge this in the courts and employment tribunal, put the government in at least a neutral light. Balls was seen as having done the right thing. In the Sonnex case the focus was different. David Scott remained a shadowy figure as far as the media were concerned and indeed resigned soon after the case (albeit under pressure from Jack Straw) so the focus of blame had to move elsewhere. This combined with the fact that probation is now firmly part of the criminal justice system, which, various forms of 'decentralisation' notwithstanding, is overwhelmingly a responsibility of central government. The result was that media focus rapidly turned to the Justice Secretary himself and his responsibility for the failure of the probation service to manage Sonnex. The *Mail* illustrates this theme:

> Demonstrating the opportunism that has been the hallmark of his political career, Jack Straw toured TV studios to apologize for the criminal negligence of Britain's justice system after two French students were tortured to death by a psychopath who should have been behind bars...If he had been truthful, 'Justice Jack' would have apologized for his government's failure to reform an incompetent justice system and then explained how he proposes to stop the terrifying growth of a feral, feckless and amoral underclass spawned by the excesses of the welfare state (Platell 2009).

Permanent moral panic

The reactions that we have described in this chapter might well be classed as examples of media-induced moral panic which Stan Cohen classically defined as a situation in which

> [a] condition, episode, person or group of persons emerges to become defined as a threat to societal values and interests; its nature is presented in a stylized and stereotypical fashion by the mass media; the moral barricades are manned by editors, bishops, politicians and other right-thinking people; socially accredited experts pronounce their diagnoses and solutions; ways of coping are evolved or (more often) resorted to; the condition then disappears, submerges or deteriorates and becomes more visible (Cohen 1972: 9).

Nigel Parton saw aspects of the Colwell case very much as a moral panic, with the proviso that the panic was started by the Inquiry, rather than the murder, itself. He argued that the press linked the inquiry established by Sir Keith Joseph to a 'wider social anxiety about the decline of the family, the growth of violence and permissiveness and concerns about the relationship between inadequate families and welfare professionals, particularly social workers' (Parton 1985: 77–78). By the time of Baby Peter and Sonnex this had widened out to embrace an entire 'feral underclass' as a threat not just to societal values but to the very security of the majority population.

This is not the place to attempt an extended discussion of theories of moral panic but there is one important issue very relevant to the discussion in this chapter. One of the problems of identifying a moral panic is knowing what would be a 'normal' and acceptable level of concern about or reaction to a phenomenon such as those we have discussed. The idea of a normal reaction presupposes, in turn, that people have some sort of access to information about the phenomenon apart from the media and by contrast to which the media can be judged to be engaged in moral panic. At the time of Maria Colwell we have noted that the media were not the only sources of information. People lived in communities and were parts of networks of neighbours and people who knew each other. As we have seen the reactions of local people to the death of Maria were not necessarily those of the national media. Indeed in some cases they were *more* severe than the national press.

Today we live in a much more fragmented society in which we are presented with a number of threatening 'others' ranging from drug addicts, the homeless, the permanently unemployed, gangs, anti-social behaviour through to terrorists, clandestine immigrants and international organised crime. The problem is that there is very little information available about the reality or otherwise of such threats from society's increasingly fragile networks of families, neighbours and workplace interaction (see Altheide 2002). As a consequence people increasingly lack a 'reliable indication of what constitutes a realistic level of concern, anxiety or alarm' (Hier 2008: 178). They become more dependent on the media for information and the media, through the vehicle of moral panic, increasingly appropriating the sense of collectivity and community in the absence of actual interactions between individuals, families, workmates and neighbours. In this sense moral panic becomes a normal feature or 'ordering practice' in modern society (Hier 2003: 19). In the next chapter this decay of community will be explored in more depth.

3
Family, Community and Violence

Both the killing of Baby Peter and the murders committed by Sonnex and Barker took place in some of the most deprived communities in Britain. In 2007 the London Boroughs of Haringey, where Baby Peter lived and brutally died, and Lewisham, where Sonnex and Farmer committed their horrific crimes, were both within the top 50 of the 354 local authorities in England on five of the six components of government measures of multiple deprivation, covering employment, incomes, health, education, housing, environment and crime (Leeser 2008).

Of course such cold statistics tell us little about the real life of poor communities. Communities, like traditional working class communities in the industrial heartlands, can be poor yet have high levels of solidarity and cohesion. But the fact is in many parts of Britain today, after decades of de-industrialisation, being poor, particularly being in the top 50 of deprived areas, is more likely to mean social isolation, social fragmentation, lack of worthwhile employment opportunities and high levels of crime and fear of crime and violence.

It is these changes in the structure of poor communities which are central to an understanding of the different circumstances in which the deaths of Maria Colwell and Peter Connelly, and the killings by Sonnex and Farmer and by Young took place. In particular the very different role of the media and their portrayal both of the incidents themselves and of the response of the social work and probation agencies, as well as the different sets of problems they actually faced in responding – and failing to respond – to these tragic events, are

45

to a considerable extent related to changes in the social structure of poor communities in the intervening years.

The traditional working class community

During the late 19th and early 20th centuries expanding industrial capitalism resulted in large cities and stable working class communities. The building of schools and factories – and prisons – in which the working class would learn the discipline of labour also laid the basis of strong community life. Strong local networks of families and workplace relations created what today would be called 'community cohesion' and 'social capital' part of which was deployed in the tasks of informal social control: the management of petty criminality and anti-social behaviour, normally by young men, and the enforcement of sexual and gender norms in the relations between men and women.

Under such conditions forms of family violence were much more publicly visible than they are today. For example in a study of wife-beating in London during the second half of the 19th century the historian Nancy Tomes characterised the situation at the beginning of the period as one in which

> tensions culminating in conflict as well as the actual beating were highly visible...it is clear that neighbours regularly watched and even participated in each other's personal quarrels (Tomes 1978: 329).

It seems permissible to assume that child abuse would have been subject to similar levels of surveillance. Sarah Wise, writing about the early history of the National Society for the Prevention of Cruelty to Children (NSPCC) – popularly known at the time as the Cruelty Men – comments:

> The Cruelty Men appear to have met with little resistance in their work, and the existing NSPCC records suggest that assaults upon inspectors were very rare...The poor seem to have acquiesced and co-operated with cruelty and neglect inspections and investigations; it was their vigilance and concern that led to the majority of the alerts to the Society in the first place. The NSPCC was har-

nessing the self-policing and inquisitiveness about neighbours that other philanthropists had already noted as a feature of slum communities (Wise 2008: 127).

Nevertheless as the 19th century progressed middle class norms penetrated working class families and violence between family members became less visible (Tomes 1978; Hammerton 1992). Intimate family relations, even for working class families with strong neighbourhood and community connections, became more privatised. In the years immediately preceding the foundation of the NSPCC in 1884, Lord Shaftesbury warned Reverend George Staite against attempting to secure child protection legislation:

> The evils you state are enormous and indisputable, but they are of so private, internal and domestic a nature as to be beyond the reach of legislation (NSPCC 2008a: 4).

Evils they nevertheless were and according to some commentators violence against children in the form of corporal punishment remained endemic to working class life right up to the 1950s. In his study of Salford during the first quarter of the 20th century Robert Roberts (1973) claims that

> it seems certain that during the early years of this century the practice was much more widespread and severe...[and that the NSPCC]...Gallantly as it worked, the Society hardly touched the fringe of the problem (Roberts 1973: 43).

Thus child protection social work arose from an understanding that to help families in the poorest working class communities the social worker had to gain access to the children in their homes, having to negotiate on doorsteps for access and often dealing with hostile or violent clients. As Ferguson (2010) notes it was important that social workers moved within people's private places and developed an understanding through experiencing the conditions and the surrounding environment in which their clients existed.

> From its beginnings in the late 19th century, social workers have walked into what have been regarded as the most unsavoury and

dangerous places in society. The investigative brief of child protection workers meant that they were at the forefront of such techniques, going into the slums to root out child cruelty (Ferguson 2010: 1105).

So the traditional working class community in the early 20th century exhibited a tension. On the one hand there were strong neighbourhoods and communities with high levels of interaction by people who knew each other through workplaces, pubs, recreation, inter-marriage and local schools. This meant that in cases of child abuse neighbours and relatives would have taken an interest and probably acquired some knowledge about the situation. On the other hand nuclear family relations in which a good deal of violence – husbands to wives, parents to children – had, over the preceding half century or so, become progressively privatised creating obstacles which the new social workers had to negotiate carefully.

The situation facing criminal justice agencies was not dissimilar. The police, after a period of conflict with the working class, learned the skills of exercising discretion, turning a blind eye to minor misdemeanours and deferring to the mechanisms of informal communal control in the expectation of co-operation on more serious criminal matters. Mike Brogden in his study of the relations between the Liverpool working class and the police at the end of the 19th century concluded that

> by the end of that period, the relations that had developed were not so much ones of consent but rather a grudging acceptance, a tentative approval that could be withdrawn instantly in the context of industrial conflict (Brogden 1982: 184).

The organised, mainly skilled sections of the working class, it is important to remember, had by this time become political actors with a growing network of trade union branches and trades councils and had founded the Labour Party. But for the poorer and unorganised, in casual employment and dependent on informal and criminal economies, a more aggressive policing remained and Roberts remarks that 'like their children, delinquent or not, the poor looked upon him [the police officer] with fear and dislike' (Roberts 1973: 100). It is here in the poorest areas that the problems of poverty and violence were most concentrated.

Nevertheless the aim of the criminal justice system as a whole by the end of the 19th century was the rehabilitation and reintegration of the working class offender into society and a life of useful labour (Garland 1985). This is the context in which the probation service emerged, originally through the police-court missionaries and initiatives by the Church of England Temperance Society to supervise drunkard offenders who came before the court. By 1894 there were 70 missionaries working to provide a system of probation as a means of reducing imprisonment and helping with rehabilitation. The Home Office originally envisaged probation officers less as a specialist service than as employees of the local magistrates, acting as intermediaries between court and community, on whose resources they would draw to socialise offenders back into law-abidingness (Nellis 2007).

The probation officer engaged closely with the working class community not simply as the world of family, work and discipline to which the rehabilitated offender was destined to return but as a key resource in bringing about that process of rehabilitation. In conjunction with voluntary and church organisations, the probation officer would be known in the community from visits to homes, schools and other institutions made in order to tap them as resources for the tasks of rehabilitation such as finding the ex-offender a job and a residence. By the 1960s this had consolidated into a spectrum of skills or 'practice wisdom' in which 'officers retained considerable leeway in what they believed and much discretion in the way they acted towards offenders' (Nellis 2007: 49). Probation officers became 'multi-skilled professionals used to the exercise of discretion and individual judgement and taking the existence of the community for granted as an essential backdrop to their work' (Fitzgibbon & Lea 2010: 221).

By the middle of the 20th century despite industrial change much of this traditional community structure still survived in the older working class areas such as the industrial North of England or the East End of London. Its most famous portrayal in British sociology was drawn in the studies by Peter Willmott and Michael Young of the Bethnal Green area of East London.

> Established residents claimed to 'know everyone'. They could do so because most people were connected by kinship ties to a network of other families, and through them to a host of friends and acquaintances. Ties of blood and marriage were local ties....

> Bethnal Green is not so much a crowd of individuals – restless, lonely, rootless – as an orderly community based on family and neighbourhood groupings (Willmott & Young 1960: 7; see also Young & Willmott 1962).

As late as 1996 Sandra Walklate (1998) in a study of levels of trust in communities in Salford, the city Roberts had portrayed 30 years earlier, was still able to find a traditional community in the 'Oldtown' dockland areas of the city. Local residents, asked about levels of trust within the community, were still able to respond with things like:

> When I'm looking round it's not for the lads or anything else, it's the dogs. I think the majority of people feel fairly safe in this area if you've lived here all the time...you know who they are (Middle-aged female, established resident).

A local police officer agreed:

> on the Oldtown estate, everybody knows each other. It's just like one big family, well not a family as such, but one tight community. A clan. That's it (Male police officer) (Walklate 1998: 556).

Colwell, Young and community

Maria Colwell lived on the Whitehawk estate in Brighton. The estate had expanded during the 1930s as a result of slum clearance of older areas of East Brighton. A local resident recalls:

> Stuck way out on the eastern fringes of the town, up a cul-de-sac valley, with little in the way of permanent employment, this has been something of a forgotten estate in the past. It was known to many city folk only through press reports of gang fights, drug busts, child abuse cases, and all the social problems that stem from high unemployment and low wage jobs (Mead 2006).

But another resident who grew up in the area in the 1950s says:

> Irrespective of what people say, Whitehawk was a great place to live in those days. People's doors were never locked and if you

wanted to get to another road the quick way, you could go through their gardens (Atkins 2007).

Even today after investment under recent government renewal programmes the estate still has a concentration of deprivation:

But even today, many children there have never seen the sea. 'That is not an urban myth, it's perfectly true; we had quite a lot of children who were scared to go off the estate and certainly plenty had never stood on the beach,' said Gill Clough, the former head teacher of Whitehawk's only secondary school, which was closed in 2003.

The case of estates like these is that the clean front doors hide very deprived interiors. There are entire generations of families who have never had a job. There is a lot of drug-taking, drinking, incest. It's one of these estates where a lot of grown men leave and you get middle-aged women hooking up with much younger men, which brings its own issues for families. Children would come to school on Monday mornings and weep – they were exposed to violence and abuse. I would say about 70 per cent of the children in my class would have quite serious issues and, of course, that was among those who came to school at all (Doward et al. 2008).

In other words Whitehawk during the mid-1970s probably lacked, as a slum clearance and then high unemployment area, many of the resources of the organised traditional working class community described above. Nevertheless what is remarkable is the presence of some of those features and some, even if residual, collective sense of solidarity and responsibility for things going on in 'our street' or 'our community'. The context in which Maria died is in many respects still evocative of the traditional community. Referring to factors which resulted in the public inquiry into her death, Nigel Parton writes:

The neighbours were heavily involved in reporting concerns to the local social services department and the NSPCC, and similar concerns were evident in the schools which she attended. A major issue was related to the failure of the appropriate agencies to respond

appropriately to these referrals and to piece the information together. In many respects it was the furore within the local community
in Brighton which provided a major impetus for establishing the
public inquiry in the first place (Parton 2004: 84).

The other side of the coin was that elements of the community
turned directly on Maria's mother.

> The word 'murderer' has been scrawled on her front wall and as
> she edged open the door today, a crowd of neighbours shouted:
> 'Come out here and we will kill you. Let's get hold of you'. They
> stood by a car on which had been stuck a poster that read 'Bring
> back hanging—especially for child murderers' (Brighton Argus,
> 18th April 1973, quoted in Drakeford & Butler 2010: 1425).

Meanwhile Maria's social worker, Diana Lees, was attacked in court
and even abused on the streets of Brighton.

> Lees was severely censured by the inquiry for various failures
> to supervise Maria when she returned to the parental home from
> foster care. The social worker became a virtual outcast in her
> own community. "I was told of Diana Lees walking through the
> streets of Brighton and being spat on," says Barnardo's operations
> director Chris Hanvey (Hanvey 2003).

The resilience of the community is not always supportive. The point
is that the Whitehawk community knew Maria and felt some sort
of direct involvement and responsibility. This hostility however
was not to any large extent the result of a media campaign as was
the case 30 years later with Baby Peter's mother, Tracey Connelly.

Meanwhile Graham Young illustrates the continued viability of
community in a somewhat different way. He committed his crimes
in Bovingdon, close to Hemel Hempstead, one of the first generation
of New Towns built after the Second World War to rehouse working
class communities from the London slums which had been decimated
during the Blitz. There was much criticism that the New Towns were
not conducive to the re-establishment of a sense of community and
by the last decade of the 20th century most were experiencing major
problems of infrastructure, housing and employment as well as high

rates of 'New Town Blues' – defined as depression and ill health stemming from a lack of community and social ties (Glancey 2006).

Nevertheless in the Young case it was taken for granted that the community felt a responsibility to enable ex-offenders to be reintegrated and rehabilitated on release from prison and local employers were seen as a resource for this purpose. Young was encouraged to work locally as he had a right to become a member of society and resume his role as citizen. He was given a job in a local factory where, as later transpired, he abused his position of trust and actually used the access it gave him to chemicals to further his poisoning career. However even his crimes reinforced a sense that he was part of the locality; his victims were locals and known to him, as he worked with them for a number of years.

The decay of community

The decline of traditional communities had been underway for some time by the time of the death of Maria Colwell and the murders committed by Graham Young. Nevertheless, as has been noted, important aspects remained and featured, in different ways, in both cases. The key issue for social work and probation became, by the early 1980s, how much of traditional community networks, as a resource for caring or for rehabilitation, actually did remain. In the early 1980s the debate focused on the issues raised by the Barclay Report (1982).

Initiated by the National Institute for Social Work at government request, the conclusion of the (majority) Report was that social work should intensify its orientation to the community by seeing one of its major tasks as activating 'the informal network' of carers.

> The Working Party believes that if social needs of citizens are to be met in the last years of the twentieth century, the personal social services must develop a close working partnership with citizens focusing more closely on the community and its strengths (Barclay Report 1982: 198).

The implication seemed to be that:

> The best strategy, in other words, for social work to adopt over the next decade or so is one that seeks to strengthen the informal

networks of carers by developing and harnessing their capacity to care (Allan 1983: 418).

Such injunctions to community hark straight back to Young and Willmott. Traditional family and community networks may be in decay but

> the Barclay Report seems to be arguing that a version of these networks can be re-created though, under contemporary urban conditions, they may need orchestrating by social workers (Allan 1983: 422).

Such an orientation was firmly rejected by one of the two 'minority' signatories to the report, Robert Pinker, a leading social policy academic, retorted that social workers were being enjoined to take on a major task of community building. He was also concerned with whether the types of relationships which existed even in traditional working class communities could easily be recruited to the type of caring roles which social work would seek to encourage.

The theme as has already been seen in the Colwell case was that community networks might not always be the benign structures assumed by Barclay. In fact the Report was not oblivious to this or to other criticisms such as the fact that most care is undertaken by women but this, in the eyes of critics, was not sufficiently reflected in the main conclusions:

> The committee, rightly, stresses both that community networks may not always be benign and that…informal care is predominantly family care, principally provided by the unpaid domestic labour of women. But the Report slides too easily…to a warmer notion of more extensive caring networks based on other ties or obligations such as friendship or neighbours in the local community. The existence, nature and the frequency of networks of this kind is not clearly demonstrated (Hallett 1983: 400).

Underlying such comments is the recognition that such informal networks of community care are in decay. In identifying the underlying social causes many commentators pointed to the geographical and social mobility resulting from sustained economic expansion of the 1950s, 1960s and early 1970s:

> with changing material circumstances – increased living standards; improved housing; greater mobility; the greater employment of married women...the basis of the solidarities described in the traditional studies have withered, and cannot in consequence be easily resurrected – even with the aid of fully trained social workers! (Allan 1983: 423).

This view saw the decline of community in working class areas as the result of economic growth and social mobility and demanded that social workers had better reconcile themselves to that fact. Apart from the awareness of such phenomena as 'New Town Blues' the decline of community was initially seen as a consequence of affluence.

Today we face a continuation of that decay but the underlying forces of economic development seem to be having very different consequences. Slowing economic growth, growing inequality and geographical segregation are now major and increasingly problematic features of British social structure. Social research supports 'the conclusion that with respect to both poverty and wealth, Britain became increasingly segregated and polarised over the past two or three decades of the 20th century' (Dorling, Rigby & Wheeler 2007: 87) and the overall tendency is that Britain 'has...become steadily more socially fragmented since 1971...the social glue and cohesion has been weakening and...Britain has been steadily moving towards a slightly more atomised society with each decade that passes' (Dorling et al. 2008: 29).

For the very poor, the communities within which the killings of Baby Peter and the murders by Dano Sonnex took place, the consequences of industrial decay have been severe. The advanced industrial economies have little need for mass industrial labour but need their members to engage primarily in their capacity as consumers (Bauman 2007). Whereas in the 1960s the growth of individualism and the decline of the cohesive working class community was seen as a product of wealth and affluence (Wilmott & Young 1960) now the same factors appear as the product of community decay under the impact of economic recession: and with very different consequences.

For the poor these have been severe. The decline of employment has taken with it a whole set of values and networks which provided status, respect, notions of adulthood and childhood and an image of a life trajectory based on school, work, marriage and family in a context of mutual recognition and support for those progressing along the same path. These have been largely replaced by insecurity, disrespect, the decline of trust, high rates of crime and violence (in the context of a decline for the country as a whole), weakening of the family and respect of young for old, and a generalised culture of individualistic narcissism.

The decay of trust was a major theme in Walklate's (1998) research. Alongside the areas of residual community cohesion she found other deprived areas characterised by social fragmentation and the decline of trust. In the 'Bankhill' district a resident said:

> I can honestly say that on that road ten years ago, that you could go down that road and you'd get all your shopping down there. All your shopping. It was a community on its own. There was everything, all the people out. You lost this community relationship, community spirit, now people don't want to know you. Like I said, you're knocking on their door and they'll think its either the police or somebody to fill them in, and they stay behind the curtains. Sad, isn't it? (Established male resident, Bankhill) (Walkate 1998: 560).

The decline of trust among local residents was a major theme and was reflected in a focus group discussion by local police officers:

> The fear amongst people in this ward…is that it could be the next door neighbour that burgles you, you're not sure who to trust. When there's no trust amongst a neighbourhood, it perpetuates. They're looking over their shoulder and they're thinking there's a fear and perhaps it doesn't even exist…these people in this ward have no trust of even their sons (Walkate 1998: 561).

Such conditions intensify the contradictions identified by critics of the Barclay report. Within social work, community fragmentation and lack of trust increases the dependence of the client on the practitioner as the sole source of assistance. At the same time the practitioner has fewer networks of knowledge of those in need in the area and how neighbours and relatives can be involved in the process of social care. This means both that clients at risk may be less easy to identify and that once a risk is identified knowledge of the client will be solely down to the actions of the practitioner and their interactions with the child's immediate family.

For the probation officer a similar set of problems arises. The reintegration of the offender into a network of viable interpersonal and family relations of a non-criminal nature becomes an almost impossible task in a community with little in the way of employment opportunities. At the same time, once the client is released into such a community the continued surveillance and monitoring of the progress of the client becomes more difficult. The location of the client at any one time becomes solely a matter for the surveillance of the probation service, possibly assisted by the police. Similar problems face the police themselves in the form of both increasing public dependence on the police as the only agency capable of tackling crime and anti-social behaviour and at the same time a lack of reporting of crime by the public due to fear of reprisals and generalised reluctance to become involved (Fitzgibbon & Lea 2010). Walklate detected this theme of the increased dependence of fragmented communities on 'the authorities' to resolve problems as community networks decline.

> The consequences, then, of this sense of loss exemplified in the view that 'This area is going downhill rapidly' appear to be twofold; on the one hand residents still reach out for 'the authorities' to do something, and on the other hand there is a sense of withdrawal from each other (Walkate 1998: 561).

Under such conditions, as illustrated by the discussion of the role of the media, what is mobilised by the media is, rather than any sense of collective responsibility and empowerment, people's fears. This enables people to be drawn in, by the media, as *virtual collective victims*. The reality of community is only achieved through a media hysteria which turns upon the agencies and their managers who have failed to protect it.

These fears spread out into society as a whole. Even for those in work insecurity is now rife. In April 2008 the Joseph Rowntree Trust undertook a public consultation via a web and postal survey of about 3,600 people (Watts 2008). In addition a number of charitable organisations working with young people, ethnic minorities and also groups whose voices are not usually heard such as those with learning difficulties, ex-offenders, people with experience of homelessness, unemployment, and care workers contributed (Mowlam & Creegan 2008).

Of the ten major social evils identified and discussed in the reports the decline in community featured prominently. It was felt that neighbours no longer knew or looked out for one another and this made people feel isolated, lonely and fearful. Many reflected on the lack of public spiritedness and social responsibility:

> People often felt that communities at the neighbourhood level have disintegrated and said things like "neighbours don't know each other" or:
> "People don't care for others, in fact it is safer to walk by on the other side of the street, people don't come into contact with each other, they are isolated by their cars and their televisions."
> One person...identified the many consequences that spring from "not living in caring communities...social isolation, depression, loneliness and the fear of personal and community safety". Another identified the following cycle: "The less people know their neighbours, the less they care about the neighbourhood and the more they feel alienated and scared" (Watts 2008: 9).

The other side of the decline of community is the growth of consumerism and individualism.

> Participants often felt that people today "see themselves only as individuals and not as part of a wider society" and this individualism was seen to be a root cause of many other social problems (Watts 2008: 9).

The report concluded that:

> Cutting across the responses is an overarching sense of unease about the rapid social changes people perceive around them. Views about today's social evils come not only from people's experi-

ences of Britain today: they are located in their perceptions of the past and expectations of the future. At the same time as recognising that these changes have brought "a mixture of good and bad effects", people are unhappy about the direction in which many of these trends have taken us. They worry about the decline of things they value – morality, community, social responsibility – and the growth of things that they feel are damaging: individualism, consumerism and greed, inequality, the misuse of drugs and alcohol (Watts 2008: 35).

Baby Peter: Isolation and family collapse

We have noted that even on the Whitehawk estate at the time of the death of Maria Colwell neighbours knew what was going on and intervened by reporting to the authorities and also taking less appropriate actions to show their disgust. Baby Peter in contrast was battered to death and no-one knew or intervened. Not only did the social workers not read the signs but the neighbours knew nothing or if they did, saw it as none of their business.

In February 2009 the charity Action for Children claimed, on the basis of a survey of a thousand adults and parents in the UK, that 'a quarter of adults in the UK have worried that a child they know may be neglected, but over a third did not act on their concerns'. The main reasons given were that they were 'frightened of repercussions or that it may cause them trouble' (16%), that 'it was not any of their business' (15%), that there was a 'lack of proof' (15%) and that they 'did not think they had enough information about who to ask for help' (23%) (Action for Children 2009).

Several important cases of child deaths by neglect or violence prior to the case of Baby Peter illustrate the tragic consequences of the breakdown in relations of trust and interaction within communities and between communities and social services. The murder of Victoria Climbié in Haringey in 2000 by her great-aunt Marie-Thérèse Kouao and Kouao's partner Carl Manning took place unnoticed by almost anyone. As Nigel Parton comments:

It is notable that, compared to the Maria Colwell case, no referrals are noted in the Victoria Climbié case from neighbours or other members of the community apart from the 'child minder' Mrs Cameron (Parton 2004: 85).

The last months of Victoria's life illustrate one aspect of the weakening of community cohesion: increased global population mobility. While immigration as such has frequently resulted in the establishment of very cohesive settled ethnic minority communities, global mobility has also resulted in an increase in short term visitors, asylum-seekers and other transients. Victoria's parents lived in the Ivory Coast and had sent Victoria to live with her great-aunt in order to improve her life opportunities. Marie-Thérèse Kouao was highly mobile with the result that Victoria was not registered at a school or with a GP. When she did appear at health or welfare departments different practitioners were often unaware that they were dealing with the same child or family.

> The impact of increased global mobility, the rapid increase in asylum-seeking families, together with the diverse backgrounds of the workers themselves, increasingly seems to characterise work in many metropolitan areas. It has a particular impact on the nature, stability and cohesion of local communities...We are not simply talking about diversity here but incredible complexity and fluidity (Parton 2004: 85).

Seven-year-old Khyra Ishaq starved to death at her home in Handsworth in 2008 at the hands of her mother Angela Gordon and the latter's partner Junaid Abuhamza. The case illustrates how the decline in surveillance by community and neighbours focuses the responsibilities on education and social services while at the same time reducing the flow of information to the latter.

> A neighbour, who described Khyra as a 'wonderful girl', hit out at the school and social services today for failing to protect her and her siblings. The man, who declined to be named, said any investigation should focus on how the tragedy was about to happen. "if they weren't going to school, the school should have known why. The school should have known something." The man, who lives a few doors away from the family, said he had not seen Khyra or her siblings for some time. "They used to be

outside having fun but I haven't seen them for about a year and a half now. I thought they might have moved" (Batty 2008).

Three-year-old Tiffany Wright who died of malnutrition and neglect in September 2007 lived above a popular Sheffield pub and was often seen by neighbours and customers who when she died acknowledged they had been concerned at how hungry and miserable she had appeared. Yet none of them had apparently acted upon their concerns. The chair of the independent review of child protection arrangements in Sheffield following Tiffany's death, in addition to criticism of the communication between agencies, said:

> I know that some neighbours and regulars at the pub were concerned about the children and knew that they were left alone from time to time. It is a matter of great regret that these concerns were not reported or acted upon (BBC News 2008).

Finally, in the case of Baby Peter, none of the neighbours reported anything to the authorities:

> Michael Gephard is 73 and has lived in the neighbourhood where Baby P died for more than 20 years..."It's not a neighbourhood and we are not neighbours," he said, walking his dog in the dark along the wet pavement. "People here come from all over – Turkey, Africa, everywhere. You might see someone move into a house with a big bag and then move out again a few months later. I know one or two people, good friends, but that's it. That little boy had his fingernails pulled out and nobody knew" (Tweedie 2008).

One aspect of the decay of communities is isolation and collapse of social networks of informal control, communication and surveillance. The other is the isolation and the collapse of the family. Just as for the middle classes in the boom years of the 1960s the decline of community was a result of affluence and mobility, increasing divorce rates and single parent families were to a considerable extent a reflection of the empowerment of women to escape violent or pointless relationships. Deprived communities today face the mirror image of this. The collapse of employment is a major factor in the collapse and increasing fragility of family relationships.

> Low-income families, especially those who reside in poverty neighbourhoods, are daily exposed to a variety of experiences that place extraordinary stress on the couple and family relationships. In addition to the constant stress of making ends meet financially, and of working in unstable, low-paying jobs, they have the frustrations of living in sub-standard housing in poorly serviced neighbourhoods, without adequate transportation, and they and their children are continually in fear of crime and violence. Members of their immediate or extended families may be struggling with depression, alcoholism or drug abuse, HIV/AIDS, or may be in and out of jail or some combination of those problems. Domestic violence is more prevalent in low-income households. Service providers who work with these couples note how often these accumulated stresses spill over into home, and anger and frustration too often poison their relationships between parents and children (Ooms 2002: 88).

The collapse of work, or the availability of only pointless poverty-wage work, not only demoralises both men and women but makes long-term marital relationships involving planning for children and home-making almost a utopian dream. This removes the incentive for long-term stable relationships. If the preceding generation of parents have also suffered from the same circumstances then this adds one more pressure towards short-term relationships between people with little or no conception of child rearing and little ability to embrace the responsibilities of parenthood.

The most intimate family relations become passing and contingent. In the case of Victoria Climbié her aunt, Ms. Kouao, moved in with her partner, Manning 'whom she had met only days before' (Masson 2006: 225). In a similar way Baby Peter's mother, Tracey Connelly, had only known her partner Steven Barker for a short time before he moved in and began abusing Peter. Meanwhile Peter's mother was obviously isolated and very vulnerable due to her own abusive background, and in many ways she sought solace and companionship through the 'virtual community' of various internet sites. On these chat sites she could be the virtual mother, feel valuable and valued and pose as a good mother who was living with a partner although in reality he was obviously predisposed to seek gratification from abusing her little boy. The real world was disconnected from her – no-one knew what was going on – while she was disconnected from the real world, transporting herself psychologically and emotionally somewhere else, disconnected from the local environment and the pain her child lived through everyday.

Sonnex: Consumerism and the criminal family

The fragmentation of community comes into play in a number of ways in the Sonnex case. Gabriel Ferez and Laurent Bonomo were visitors to London. They had lived for three months in the area when Sonnex and Farmer struck. In traditional communities new arrivals would be immediately noticed and either welcomed or, as frequently was the case with people of a different ethnicity, be shunned as a threat. But they would be *known*. The two French students on short-term placement were unaware of the dangers within the area where the Sonnex family were very well known (including to the police and probation service) as violent and criminal. But just as no-one knew what was happening to Baby Peter, no-one warned the students of any possible risks or indeed was even aware of the presence of these two visitors to the area.

But at a more fundamental level the collapse of meaningful work in such areas leaves only consumption as a source of gratification and identity. For the middle classes and the rich this consumption as 'lifestyle choice' becomes a form of spurious liberation. In such a world however the poor remain as only the 'flawed consumers' (Bauman 1998: 91) while the massive presence of consumption all around through the media and the city intensifies the feeling of relative deprivation and leads many young people in deprived areas, freed from the constraints of community and trust, to become ultra-consumers in a fantasy world. The same isolation from the real world which led Tracey Connelly onto the internet as a 'virtual good mother' may well have led Dano Sonnex and Nigel Farmer to a fantasy world of consumption. The criminologists Steve Hall, Simon Winlow and Craig Ancram in their study of young people and crime in the North East of England explain the dynamics in the following way:

> the dependable structures of gendered identity that ordered these communities during the industrial modern period had been transformed into tangled web of narcissism, egoism, uncertainty and anxiety, framed against an imposing background of advanced consumer symbolism. Immediately striking here was the number of adult young men who had powerful bodies and brutal attitudes towards others, yet who also displayed an almost childlike fascination with youth-oriented clothes, gadgets and media production. For those we spoke to, life was understood as a constant battle for cultural significance in the locale and in a fantasised version of the broader culture...In the vast majority of cases the lives of our respondents were dominated by the constant scramble to accumulate and display, and many had become enchanted by an idealised image of themselves that bore no relationship at all to the actual material and socio-political realities of their lives (Hall et al. 2008: 29–30).

Although both offenders were high on drugs and obviously wanted money for more drugs their anger and rage was probably compounded because of the nature of the people they were attacking. These foreign students symbolised to them the opportunities and consumer goods that they lacked: the opportunity to travel, to be educated, to achieve high-level employment and therefore a legitimate way of making good money. Sonnex, from his deprived abusive background and poor education, may have been triggered into an extremely violent attack not only by his drug misuse but by the fact that in the face of these two successful strangers he saw his own image as flawed consumer.

But Sonnex was not without family of sorts. He came in fact from one of the most notorious criminal families in the area. Criminal families reflect, however, the communities within which they operate. The traditional, cohesive, communities of the East End of London spawned criminal families like the Krays and in South London the Richardsons. These criminal groups, active in the 1960s, although capable of extreme violence, had a certain level of integration into their communities. They sought respect as well as fear. They sometimes saw it as their task to enforce what they considered popular morality. People would on occasion go to them to 'sort out' problems. Young petty criminals would grow up with a respect for these local families and even the police would establish various forms of accommodation (Hobbs 1988; Foster 1990). These were carefully distinguished from (using an old football analogy) the 'league division three' criminals. A police officer in Foster's study described the hierarchy:

> The average villain in this area had a lot of respect for us. We're on the other side of the fence but it's a game...They're honest in as much as you know where you stand with them. League division three criminals you have problems with. They are the types who hit back, the ones who will never accept nothing...you don't know where you stand, you gotta watch yer back the whole time. If I know where I stand that makes all the difference. Funny thing to say about a villain but it's the only way I can adequately describe it (Foster 1990: 19).

As the old communities declined under the impact of migration and industrial change so the old crime families lost their social status. While the lucrative criminal activities became internationalised local criminal organisations became more disorganised and violent. The Sonnex family was from such a background and while not the type of temporary liaison exemplified by Connelly and Barker, was very much held together by criminality and violence.

The family were of the type that the older 'first division' criminals would have employed from time to time to do their dirty work but at the same time would keep at arm's length because of the 'unreliability' that was a consequence of their potential for uncontrolled violence. For these 'third division' criminal gangs and families the only route to status and 'respect' was fear and violent aggression which extended to their relations with the police and with other people in the surrounding area: the war of all against all. Such gangs and families become all the more powerful as communities fragment and decay. Isolated individuals are more easily intimidated. There is no social network of family and community which might include some 'friendly' local villains who might 'sort out' excessively violent individuals where the police fail to do so.

Daniel Sonnex grew up with violence, both domestic and against strangers, all around him. His father, Bernard Sonnex, had served six prison sentences for 47 crimes, including firearms and drug offences. His elder brother Bernie served ten sentences for 34 offences and was returned to prison in 2009 on a sentence for aggravated burglary. His sister Louise was imprisoned for attacking another woman with a golf club and in 2005 was jailed for attacking a woman in a pub brawl with a broken glass (see Bird 2009). Finally, Dano Sonnex himself, as we know, was jailed in 2003 for eight years for violent robberies of which sentence he served five years and four months before his release on licence after which he committed a further serious offence prior to unleashing his frenzy of violence on the two French students. The notoriety of the Sonnex family makes it all the more incomprehensible that he was not under more stringent control by probation.

Social work and probation without community

So when such terrible mindless crimes as those committed by Sonnex and by Barker take place local people are reminded of their own impotence and the fact that they no longer live in a community. The frustration leads to a temporary feeling of solidarity through moral outrage, mobilised through the media, and directed at the 'authorities' who manifestly failed in their task of protection. This is the first and perhaps the most powerful effect of social isolation and the decline of community on the work of practitioners. They are the first target for blame.

> People can't manage what they did to the child [*Baby Peter*] it's so awful to think about that situation – the best way to deal with that is to focus your anger somewhere else. You can't focus your anger on these people because you don't understand them, how can that happen, I don't really understand that, right so who should have prevented that and then they just focus on that, again because it's just too difficult. It's distancing yourself away from people, because people feel they can't allow themselves to think that human beings have that capability. You project your anger on to something else. Often it gets mixed up with people's own feelings, like the whole Diana thing, like a mass

hysteria. We've gone from a country that was very repressed about death and we were suddenly being allowed to be very emotional, publicly display emotion, people weeping and wailing, they kept weeping and wailing for her, there was a displacement of emotions. I feel that's what happens with these high profile cases. *Pippa – Social Work Manager*

There has been a change, it's being the old chestnut being a blame culture now and much more of a witch hunt mentality when it comes to, for example, the whole Baby P case, where the media whips up a real frenzy – the focus is taken away from the people who actually perpetrate the abuse and moved on to the practitioner...I'm not taking away the emphasis from the things we need to learn from that and from the things that go wrong and should have happened but I feel there's much more of an emphasis on blaming those ills on people that are tryingto help or prevent them than the people individuals that do the abuse themselves. Looking back I think there were those kinds of responses in the past but it seems that they have increased over time. *Kristy – Social Worker*

However, the paradox is that the same process of community decay which exaggerates public expectations of the agencies makes it harder for the latter to function effectively. This is clear in examining the way in which public collaboration is in fact crucial to the local functioning of social work and criminal justice agencies, at least in their traditional forms. For the police it has been understood for some time that public trust and confidence leading to the flow of information from the community about crime is crucial for police effectiveness (Lea & Young 1984; Kinsey et al. 1986). For probation not only is the community important as a resource for rehabilitation and desistance but also in the simple role of surveillance as, for example, with public sightings of probation clients violating the terms of their release or parole. These may be reported to probation or via the police and this enables the system to function and stand a better chance of avoiding the sort of mistakes exemplified by the Sonnex murders. For social services observations and concerns by neighbours regarding the condition of children or persons in need of care is a crucial resource.

So both the probation officer and social worker traditionally relied on a real link with the local community and awareness that to understand the problems facing their clients they had to understand the context and environment in which those clients lived. As two of the more experienced interviewees recounted:

> You followed things up, you got to know people and you helped enormously, in terms of helping to solve crises for people. Even just getting people the money they were entitled to. I remember getting a disabled woman and her son £3,000 in back pay for pension she was entitled to. It didn't take me long but there was a sense you worked with the community, with the family. You worked with whatever was important to the offender, you are there temporarily, you put in an amount and those resources will be there, when the probation order is over. You recognized the importance of getting close to the offender but also keeping a professional distance and I learned that a lot working in the community. Taking them away in groups helped them integrate and get on better with each other.
> *Marvin – Probation Manager*

> Less and less people do home visits, they have lost the skills in what to look for, what to look for when you go in someone's home. Looking for the obvious; you're looking for children's toys in a sex offender's house. You're looking for the obvious and that's what people think. But now you're looking for other signs like are people's walls broken where people have smashed plates against them and various other bits and pieces but that's forgotten about. And I struggle with the fact that we've actually got staff now that don't know what to look for on a home visit.
> *Lucy – Probation Officer*

Changes such as the embracing of the risk agenda, targets and the 'tick-box' approach are seen as state driven, flowing from the adoption by recent governments of such strategies as New Public Management, the deskilling of practitioners and the changed status of managers will be addressed in Chapter 5. But what is also important is the effect that the changes in the structure of community and family networks in the poorest areas of our cities have had on the work of practitioners. If the target and tick-box orientation has resulted in the pulling of the practitioner away from the client and their social networks towards the computer screen and the risk assessment form, there has been an equally important push from the collapse of those traditional networks and interactions which made it possible for the practitioner to have a real and complex engagement with the community.

The idea of the probation officer activating community resources to find their client suitable employment and accommodation, or the social worker activating community resources of information and caring to help families in need, becomes far more difficult where those resources are scarce or non-existent and where those relations that do exist are in large part those of the street gang or the market-place of criminal opportunities. The retreat to the risk assessment and the ticking of boxes is an easy exit from the complexities of working in such an environment and one in which the front line practitioner frequently has little choice.

The growing distance from involvement with the community in which the client or offender moves changes the form of knowledge that the practitioner has of the client. Nigel Parton (2008) identifies a shift from 'social' to 'informational' knowledge, the latter derived increasingly from risk assessment databases rather than from a know-ledge of the client in their social networks and contexts. As a senior probation manager put it:

> We're better as an organisation at sharing and communicating than we were. But there's still something missing and that is the real genuine understanding of the offender. So we might be sharing information about the extent to which an offender is reporting to see us, we might be listening to comments from the police that he's been seen...he's sleeping on someone else's floor...that he's not living where he used to. We don't work out what that means, we don't analyse that and ask ourselves...if he's sleeping on his friend's sofa and he's been telling me other-wise or if he's been seen to be associating with certain people or if he's been injured in a fight, we're not thinking about what does that mean, let's ask him more, how can we find out... understand...what's actually going on. *Philip – Senior Probation Manager*

Harry Ferguson (2010) talks, in the context of a discussion of child protection, of the need for practitioners to maintain the skills of finding out what is actually going on in the client's environment. Practitioners need to 'walk the walk':

> by looking around homes, walking towards children to properly see, touch, hear and walk with them to ensure they are fully engaged with and safe, here and now, on this home visit, or in this clinic or hospital ward (Ferguson 2010: 1100).

This, as the comments about home visits cited above suggest, is a dying art and much of the pressure comes from the locality itself in areas where 'walking the walk' requires (metaphorically speaking) body armour or a mobile phone link to the office for safety.

Social policy can respond to these developments in two ways. It can effectively sidestep the issue by denying a major role for community networks in the solution to social problems such as crime, family breakdown and child neglect. Or it can take steps to develop a coherent policy for community renewal. Recent governments seem to have been in various ways engaged in both.

The removal of the offender or problem family from any link to community networks was one consequence of neo-conservative theorising about the poor as an underclass of people with a different set of values from the rest of society (see Murray 1984; Wilson 1987; Lister ed. 1996). It followed that criminality or family failure was a product of this separate subculture which reproduced itself irrespective of social conditions in poor communities; indeed it was partly responsible for them. This made way for the essentially neo-liberal assumption that individuals were entirely responsible for their own life courses – including criminality or the failure to form stable family relations. From this is derived a focus on the moral responsibility of the offender for making the 'wrong choices' and failing to manage their 'criminogenic needs'. The offender is thereby devoid of any context in which perhaps some forms of criminality make sense as a way of responding to circumstances. The aim of agencies like probation becomes that of getting offenders to manage their 'criminogenic needs' in a way which is disconnected from strategies to help reintegrate the offender into community life. Such thinking constitutes a dangerous influence on probation practitioners in their new role as 'offender managers':

> What we object to is the language of hostility and aggression – or warfare – which has been increasingly used not just to describe what probation officers are supposed to do but how the public at large are meant to feel about offenders...The probation service will contribute to this process if it does not successfully resist the current pressure to deny that offenders too are citizens, members of some community and have claims upon us by virtue of their membership (Smith & Stewart 1997: 105).

On the other hand a major focus of New Labour policy inspired by Tony Blair has been concerned with 'community cohesion' and renewal. A problem here has been that much cohesion policy has reinforced the marginalisation of the poor by resorting to criminal justice methods aimed at recreating a community spirit through the exclusion of troublesome groups by a variety of legal devices of which the most well known became the Anti-Social Behaviour Order (ASBO) (see Squires and Stephen 2005). For the excluded there is hardly anything in the way of community. Anna Minton (2009) describes a Friday night in Salford for young people:

> The few pubs we passed...had signs outside barring anybody under twenty-five. On the evening I visited, the Beacon Centre, a £1 million facility for young people, was shut and the owner was locking up at Oliver's Gym. Most young people like to go out with friends at the weekend, but Graham [a local youth worker] told me there is nothing to do here. 'Five or six years ago the pubs in Salford stopped letting eighteen-year-old kids in. Friday night in a city like Salford and there's nothing for them to do. They have to go into the bushes with a six pack and then they go out onto the streets because they feel strangled. The city centre would be all right but they don't go because they don't have the money for that kind of night out...' The result is that 'the intoxication is a bit different because they're running in and out the

bushes with the police behind them,' he said (Minton 2009: 160–161).

Sadly the situation is very similar to that in Leeds described by Nick Davies in his interview with youngsters in deprived areas of Leeds over ten years earlier:

> They all had their own dreams, most of them very mundane. They wanted to go to college, to get a job or simply to have something to do all day. In real life, as they readily described, there were only two things to do – thieving and twocking [car stealing]. They wanted much more. Their lives refused to let them have it, so they became frustrated and hopeless and bitterly angry. And they fought their war against the law with a furious rage (1997: 82).

Thus much social policy 'has become less about socially integrating those who live at the margins of society and more about guarding the boundaries between the established and the outsiders' (Rodger 2008: 165). The new coalition government following the general election of May 2010 intends to review such measures as the ASBO on grounds of their ineffectiveness, a point which was made graphically by the sociologist Richard Sennett:

> Blair thought social behaviour could be "reformed" top-down ...[but]...cultures hold together or fall apart for reasons that transcend power. On the housing estate in Chicago where I lived as a child, frail African-American grandmothers and Italian grandfathers issued something like ASBOs and these were likely to be obeyed: the grandparents commanded a moral authority which no policeman or social worker will ever possess. Of the 17,000 ASBOs issued from 2000 to 2008, 55% have been breached, so the new government is looking for something else (Sennett 2010).

On the other hand massive cuts in public spending and public sector employment, and cuts in housing benefits which threaten to drive large numbers of the poor out of city centres do not bode well for a social policy aimed at the restoration of viable community life in the poorest areas.

Yet viable community life is essential for probation and social work to function effectively. In the context of probation work, as a number of studies have suggested, successful desistance from offending is less to do with psychiatric treatment or 'managing criminogenic needs' but rather involves offenders responding to opportunities in the outside world: such as finding employment or getting married (Maruna & Immarigeon 2004; Vanstone 2004b). A recent study suggested that currently fashionable orientations to cognitive skills in learning to self-manage criminogenic needs 'would have appeared to have had little impact upon the resolution of obstacles by probationers' (Farrall 2004: 201). Rather, 'as probationers gained work, were reunited with family members or developed attachments to new partners or children, so they refrained from behaviours likely to result in offending' (Farrall 2004: 199, see also Farrall 2007).

From the standpoint of social work more generally, the issues raised are those that were raised by the Barclay Report in 1982, namely the relation of the practitioner to the process of trying to build and revive community networks. In an important way the radical implications of the Barclay Report have now become clear: only by engaging in community activism will social workers and probation officers help create the conditions under which problem families can be surveyed and helped by local caring networks and ex-offenders can find activities leading to desistance rather than a return to crime. This requires the re-activation of traditional social work skills focused on the ability to acquire in-depth knowledge of the way an offender or a problem family thinks and relates to such people, networks and opportunities as may exist. It also requires a measure of political engagement with the issues of community survival under the harsh conditions of the post welfare-state. Such political issues demand a much longer discussion but would imply at least the revival of some aspects of earlier 1970s traditions of radical social work (see Bailey & Brake 1975). Perhaps practitioners need to, as Chris Jones puts it, 'pay more attention to the wider socio-economic environment which influences and shapes the major political parties' (Jones 2001: 560).

How would such developments have made any difference to the life of Baby Peter or to the orgy of killing by Dano Sonnex? Obviously such questions are hypothetical but it is nevertheless possible to speculate on the basis of what has been said about older more cohesive poor communities. First, Baby Peter: his troubled appearance might have been picked up by neighbours and reported to social services or other agencies and the relationship between Connelly and Barker would have been under greater surveillance. Barker's Rottweiler might have provoked neighbours to complain: neighbours who said nothing, who felt isolated and vulnerable to intimidation might have had more courage to act, feeling that they had support.

Similarly, neighbours in such a community might have been more curious about the arrival of two middle class French students in their midst. They might have warned them to steer clear of the Sonnex family who were 'bad news'. In such a community also even the criminal violence of the Sonnex family might have been subject to some form of local community sanctions of the 'not on your own doorstep' variety. From the point of view of probation supervision when Sonnex came out of prison, surveillance would have probably been more effective, and an experienced probation officer equipped with the old casework skills celebrated in the old probation service slogan 'advise, assist and befriend' might have found it just possible to get even Dano Sonnex interested in doing something else.

4
Political Responses and Inquiries

Serious cases of failure by agencies such as social services and probation necessarily result in some sort of panel of inquiry. Inquiries may be seen as instruments of rational policy-making and organisational adjustment. Depending on the level at which they take place and the wideness of their remit, they may be aimed simply at finding out what in a particular case went wrong and why, where responsibility lies and what sanctions, if any, or organisational 'tweaking' are necessary to minimise the likelihood of recurrence. On the other hand they may, usually under the leadership of a knowledgeable outsider, be charged with looking at the extent to which the failure in question reflects fundamental policy orientations or organisational structure and working of the agencies involved, and recommend far reaching changes.

Putting things right

The Maria Colwell Committee of Inquiry (1974) chaired by Thomas Field-Fisher QC was uniquely a public inquiry; indeed it owed its existence to local pressure from neighbours and others. The murders committed by Graham Young featured in two inquiries both concerned with the issue of mentally disordered offenders (MDOs). The main investigation, chaired by Judge Carl Aarvold (Aarvold et al. 1973), was concerned with the specific details of the Young case while the committee under Lord Butler (Home Office & DHSS 1975) focused on changes in the law.

The first important aspect to note is the radically different environment in which they took place in comparison with that at the time of the Baby Peter and Sonnex cases. Although the Colwell inquiry, as previously noted, was to a considerable extent the result of public pressure and there was even jostling of some of the witnesses as they arrived at the inquiry – notably Pauline Kepple – there was nothing remotely resembling the media campaign that surrounded the Baby Peter and Sonnex cases. Issues of crime and justice were generally low on the political agenda (Downes & Morgan 1997) until at least the late 1970s. The same could be said of child protection. Although there was growing concern, following the Colwell inquiry, about issues of family breakdown, the notion of a feral underclass threatening social stability was largely absent.

Both inquiries had therefore more space for calm deliberation outside the glare of publicity than is the case nowadays. There are gains and losses. The loss is an immediate politicisation of issues while the gain is a much greater public scrutiny and accountability in matters which were previously regarded as the preserve of a patrician elite of experts. The Colwell inquiry was in fact, as a public inquiry, followed by the national press but, as we have noted, in a fairly restrained manner. A relatively calm atmosphere therefore remained in which an elite of professionals and experts could deliberate, learn what went wrong and devise policies to avoid future recurrence. This brings us to the second important aspect: that although the allocation of blame and the documentation of failure was an aspect of the inquiries it was subordinate to these wider concerns. Ministers in particular, Sir Keith Joseph in the Colwell case and Reginald Maudling in the Young case, awaited the conclusion of these inquiries and then formulated policy as they saw fit. High profile pre-emptive moves involving the dismissal of senior officials probably never occurred to them.

Despite criticism of Maria's designated social worker, Diana Lees, the Colwell inquiry stressed the shared responsibility of all agencies for the failure of communication between agencies – one of the main conclusions of the inquiry.

> Whilst we entirely accept that a heavy responsibility for passing on and eliciting information to these 'other agencies' rests on social services departments, we must nonetheless stress that this should not be a one-way process and that the social workers may reasonably expect that matters of concern about individual

families or children will be passed on to them by these agencies whether or not they have already indicated their interest to them. The problem of communication is a complex one, resting as it does on a combination of formal and informal arrangements, of administrative systems and direct personal contact.... there were many times when the social workers concerned with Maria simply did not know who else was involved and the nature of that involvement (Field-Fisher 1974: 62).

Indeed, the historical importance lies in its focus on the need for better liaison and communication between the agencies involved in child protection. 'What has clearly emerged is a failure of the system compounded of several factors of which the greatest and most obvious must be that of the lack of...communication and liaison' (Field-Fisher 1974: 62). As we shall see one of the most important questions still at the present time both in social work and probation is the problem of effective communication between agencies, a problem that seems impervious to a simple or, to date, any solution.

Nigel Parton (2004) makes an important comparison between the Colwell inquiry and the inquiry by Lord Laming into the death of Victoria Climbié in 2000 (see below) only a couple of years before Baby Peter.

There were major systematic failures in relation to Maria Colwell, but primarily concerning the sharing of information and the failure of professionals in different agencies to liaise. More specifically, the report identified the failure to communicate and liaise between two workers, one from the NSPCC [National Society for the Prevention of Cruelty to Children] and one from social services, as absolutely crucial in the final 8 months of Maria's life. It was the failure of these two workers to liaise with each other and to involve others, preferably via a case conference, which was seen as key to the final outcome.

The failures of communication and interagency collaboration seem much more complex in the Climbié Inquiry. These problems appear to be located: between workers; between frontline workers and first-line managers; between different professionals and workers in different organisations and agencies, whether these be social services, health or police, and to a lesser extent the NSPCC; between senior managers and their employees; and between senior managers themselves. Similarly, we are not talking only of verbal communication and written records but of the whole system of exchanging information and the way information is collated and gathered on a variety of sophisticated yet inadequate information systems. The examples of failures with information data systems are many and varied in the report. Rather than aiding communication, such systems seem to both complicate and make things worse (Parton 2004: 87–88).

Indeed it is true to say that inter-agency collaboration began with the Colwell inquiry report recommendations (see Burke 1996). The problem has, however, not been resolved: rather it has become more complex.

One final contrast with the more recent cases is that the Colwell inquiry went out of its way to ensure that none of the practitioners involved could be accused of not having performed according to the best of their ability:

Nevertheless it must be realized that the relative importance of certain of those errors only becomes obvious with the advantage of hindsight and moreover, it is impossible to conceive of any human activity in which human, and perfectly understandable, fallibility does not play a part...There was no question at any time in our view of anyone deliberately shirking a task; there was no shortage of devotion to duty (Field-Fisher 1974: 86).

Indeed, for one member of the inquiry team, Olive Stevenson, this had not been given sufficient stress. She disagreed, in a dissenting note, with what she saw as unjust criticism of social workers and stressed that even the community must shoulder some of the blame itself:

of the many of the Brighton residents who came forward at the inquiry few had voiced their anxieties, to the appropriate persons at the material times. It is most disturbing to contemplate the amount of concern and anxiety about Maria which never reached Miss Lees (Field-Fisher 1974: 8).

Maria's social worker Diana Lees, despite having been a target of physical attack during her evidence sessions, told a post-publication press conference that she regarded the inquiry report as 'reasonably fair'. The British Association of Social Workers, monitoring its press coverage, concluded that 'the overall standard of reporting and editorialising in the national press on the Maria Colwell affair was fair and sympathetic' (Community Care 1974 quoted by Butler & Drakeford 2010: 1423). The contrast with events following the death of Baby Peter could not have been greater.

The Aarvold committee which looked into the murders committed by Graham Young while on licence from Broadmoor was not a public inquiry and was far more a gathering of lawyers and criminal justice and medical professionals who would present their conclusions to the political authorities. Blame, let alone sackings or forced resignations, were simply not on the agenda of either Reginald Maudling the Home Secretary or in fact the Aarvold committee itself. Although there had been some criticism of the probation service during the inquiry, the published report simply acknowledged that 'the case was dealt with in accordance with the procedures accepted at the time to ensure proper weight was given to questions of public safety' (Aarvold et al. 1973: 1).

Two aspects of the report of the Aarvold inquiry are worthy of comment. First, as with the Colwell Inquiry, a major focus was the failure of liaison between different agencies, in this case probation, police and the medical authorities at Broadmoor. It had transpired that Young's offence history and illness were not disclosed to his supervising probation officer before his release in February 1971. Therefore any criticism of probation supervision had to acknowledge that the supervising officer never received sufficient details regarding Young's history or the risk he posed. As Herschel Prins has observed:

questions arise about the adequacy of supervision by his supervisors (to be fair to the probation service, they claim they were not given adequate information about Young's past history); it has been suggested that he was never visited in his lodgings.

When the police went there following his arrest they found a variety of chemicals and bizarre drawings of men in various stages of dying, including some pictures of them with hair loss – a feature of thallium poisoning (Prins 1999: 79).

The Inquiry felt that to avoid future recurrence in a similar case,

the social worker who is likely to supervise him, and the local consultant who will be taking over responsibility for the medical aspect of treatment if the patient is going to an area distant from the treating hospital, should be brought into consultation at an early stage. Not only will this enable the decision about discharge to be taken with the best possible knowledge of the likely circumstance, but it will allow time for the patient and those who will be concerned in the follow up process to become acquainted with each other and the problems which they will be facing (Aarvold et al. 1973: 15).

The framework for this should be an extended use of case conferences involving professionals from the various relevant disciplines whose assessments would take into consideration:

Assessment of individual patient's personality, the nature of his mental disorder, his response to therapeutic help, the circumstances, both material and emotional in which the offence took place, the likelihood of those circumstances recurring, the resources available in the social situation the patient would go to on leaving hospital, the likely reaction to that situation, and the chances of his successful reintegration in the community despite any stresses which may develop (Aarvold et al. 1973: 8).

This brings us to the second feature of the Aarvold inquiry worthy of comment which is the assumptions made about risk and public protection. The aim of the Aarvold inquiry (and the subsequent Butler inquiry) was, in the words of a contemporary commentator, the 'maintenance of a balance between what is best for those [mentally disordered offenders] guilty of dangerous offences and the right of the public to be protected' (Rolin 1976: 159). It was this balance which would hopefully be achieved by better liaison through case conferences. Today the idea that the requirements of public protection need to be balanced by the rights of the offender, particularly if convicted of dangerous offences, to be rehabilitated might seem outlandish but in the mid-1970s rehabilitation was still a major aim of those agencies, such as probation, concerned with the management of offenders.

Post-political governance and hysteria

In the recent cases of Baby Peter and Dano Sonnex the image of the appropriate ministers calmly waiting to consider the conclusions of inquiries by experts before carefully formulating policy is anything but accurate. It is not that this process has ceased. In child protection the reports of the inquiries conducted by Lord Laming following the death of Victoria Climbié and then again following the murder of Baby Peter made recommendations which have led to policy developments. Probation was to an extent shielded from the necessity to submit to anything similar to the Laming inquiry by virtue of its tighter integration into the criminal justice system, much more an organ of the central state than local authority social services. Thus the inquiries in the wake of the Sonnex affair were conducted by the faceless bureaucrats of Her Majesty's Inspectorate of Probation rather than a publicly visible member of the House of Lords.

But there were other differences. Unlike the Colwell and Young cases those of Baby Peter and Sonnex followed closely on the heels of very similar incidents. Baby Peter followed the death of Victoria Climbié in 2000 in remarkably similar circumstances, a death which had already prompted government to initiate a major inquiry by Lord Laming into child protection. The fact that Baby Peter died in the same borough, Haringey, as Victoria Climbié gave an added sense of urgency. London probation faced a similar situation regarding the Sonnex murders. In 2005 a banker (John Monckton) was murdered by Damien Hanson who was at the time on parole after serving six years of a 12 year prison sentence for attempted murder and conspiracy to rob, and Elliot White who was subject to a Drug Treatment and Testing Order (DTTO) for six months for possession of cocaine (HM Inspectorate of Probation 2006b). Again in 2006 Anthony Rice murdered Naomi Bryant while on parole after serving

15 years of a life sentence for attempted rape (HM Inspectorate of Probation 2006a). These incidents gave an added urgency to the investigations into the Sonnex murders.

But the most important difference by far was the fact that such inquiries took place in a very different political and social context. The fallout from the media hysteria surrounding both the Baby Peter and the Sonnex cases included high profile, precipitate action by government ministers against senior managers: Sharon Shoesmith, head of Haringey Social Services and David Scott, head of London Probation Area.

To understand these events it is first necessary to stand back and view some of the profound changes that have taken place in the role of both social services and probation in the period between Colwell/Young and Baby Peter/Sonnex. The previous two chapters have given a broad account of some of the socio-economic changes as they impact on the structure of communities and the relations between public and the mass media. Here we can add reference, albeit very briefly, to two key policy and political developments which are ultimately part of the same dynamic of change.

1.   From welfare to security

Unlike during the early 1970s crime and violence are now high on the political agenda. Despite recent falls in actual crime levels, public concern and fear of crime remains at high levels. Part of that fear is, as previously noted, a fear of a 'feral underclass' of permanently unemployed social deviants who are regarded, by the middle class tax paying public in particular, less as fellow citizens in a comprehensive universalist welfare state than as a 'risk group' or dangerous population against which it is the duty of the state to provide security and protection.

In criminal justice terms such developments imply what David Garland (2001) has referred to as the decline of *penal welfare*. For our purposes this can be simply illustrated by reference to the fact that the notion which preoccupied the Aarvold and Butler inquiries, that the protection of the public and the rehabilitation of the offender are equally valid and important aspects of policy which pull in different directions and between which some balance must be found, has been displaced by public protection as the overwhelmingly predominant task of criminal justice. In the political programme of the previous, New Labour, government this was epitomised by the title of the 2002 White Paper *Justice For All* (which declared the aim of government policy to be 'to rebalance the system in favour of victims, witnesses and communities' (Home Office et al. 2002: 3).

The detailed implications of this policy and other developments for probation will be considered in the next chapter. What is important here is the fact that the primacy of public protection had a particular effect on probation (and also on social services). In the context of greater public dependence on these services discussed in the preceding chapters, the 'over-selling the promise of public protection poses serious risks for offender management services by creating a dynamic that drives up consumer demand for more controlling and incapacitating measures' (McCulloch & McNeill 2007: 223). At the same time it raises the costs of failure: the public must be absolutely protected at all times. Given the 'uncomfortable truth that the potential for the commission of serious further offences cannot be eradicated' (Burke 2009: 221), the likelihood of major public and media backlash against probation when failures do occur is enhanced.

Similar issues apply in child protection social work.

> The government, they set up society with huge expectations which is politics. There is no way anybody can meet them and then when you don't meet them the reaction is, isn't this terrible, this is unacceptable, let's blame someone. I think sometimes social workers are their own worst enemies in terms of how they portray themselves. We allow ourselves to be a bit of a punch bag. We just sit and take it – a lot of the time. *Pippa – Social Work Manager*

Writing in the wake of the murder of Baby Peter, Harry Ferguson argued:

> The entire commentary on the case has been based on a key assumption – that it is possible for social work intervention to protect all children from abuse and, ultimately, death. Yet this idea is questionable and is in fact quite new...
>
> Ironically, at a time when further improvements in practice meant that deaths in child protection work became a rare event,

managing the risk of system failure, rather than learning from and celebrating success, became the defining approach.

The central paradox of modern child protection is that the better social workers have become at protecting children and preventing their deaths, the more bitter the public and political outcry has become when this fails to happen (Ferguson 2008).

None of this is to imply that the particular cases of Baby Peter or Sonnex were not avoidable tragedies: they were. The point is a more general one: that the increasing demand for infallibility in public protection has occurred in the context of the progressive deskilling and declining professional status of large parts of probation and social work as a result of the regime of targets and formulaic risk assessments resulting from New Public Management-inspired changes in these agencies. The political writer David Marquand has described eloquently the effect of neo-liberal critiques of the expertise of professionals:

For the marketisers, the professional, public service ethic is a con. Professionals are self-interested rent-seekers, trying to force the price of their labour above its market value. The service ethic is a rhetorical device to legitimise a web of monopolistic cartels whose real purpose is to rip off the consumer. There is no point in appealing to the values of common citizenship. There are no citizens: there are only customers. Public servants cannot be trusted to give of their best…Like everyone else, they can be motivated only by sticks and carrots. If possible, privatisation must expose them to the sticks and carrots of market competition. If not, they must be kept on their toes by repeated audits, assessments and appraisals (Marquand 2004: 3).

Again, the details will be discussed in the next chapter. What is important to understand here is that the combination of the declining status of probation officers and social workers from part of a respected body of skilled professions to overworked and underpaid 'public protection' security guards and the increasing demands of the public and the media for absolute protection is bound to produce a situation in which failures, however small in number, give rise to high profile media panics. To this toxic mix must be added a final ingredient: the changed nature of politics.

2. The hollowing out of democracy

Referring to such phenomena as increasingly low voter turnout at elections, declining membership of political parties, some political scientists have argued that we are witnessing 'the twin processes of popular and elite withdrawal from mass electoral politics' (Mair 2006: 25). The convergence of the programmes of the major parties have blurred political ideologies and strong linkages to social groups and interests. So people see politics as having less impact on their lives. This is particularly true of younger people (Franklin 2004). Add to this the fragmentation of poor communities and their social networks and the greater reliance on the media for a sense of collectivity and for information and we can see how media moral panics to a considerable extent have become a substitute for the articulation of political opinions and interests.

Meanwhile governments themselves have increasingly sought a 'direct' relationship with the population unmediated by parties and the clash of interests but relying increasingly on opinion polls, focus groups and, of course, the mass media. This was the factor, according to Mair (2006), that lay behind Tony Blair's increasingly 'presidential' style of leadership in which policies would often be announced to the media before being announced and discussed in parliament.

The upshot is that ministers pay increasing attention to the media rather than the political process. This dictates a quick, high profile reaction to events. The space in which parliament, let alone specialist inquiries, can deliberate and formulate policy *before* ministers have acted is turned on its head. It is the quick, often hastily conceived reaction of ministers in the media which then sets the terms for, and may activate, other pressures upon the various inquiries which may follow. Combine these changes with those already mentioned – the public demand for total protection and the deskilling and decline of professional status of both managers and practitioners in probation and social services – and we have the ingredients for the high profile ministerial reactions which followed the Baby Peter and Sonnex incidents and which more generally in the New Labour administration 'allowed rhetorical toughness rather than reason and evidence to dominate both guiding principles and policy' (Vanstone 2010: 284; see also Fulwood 2010).

I feel the government are so swept away with public opinion and the press, pretty much the press to me determines. What the government doesn't seem to be able to do is separate itself from the press...and...has to be seen to have responded in a way that placates the masses. Rather than actually saying 'no we are going to go away and think about what did happen', is this actually fair? They are just reactive; the press has whipped up the public, the government need a sacrificial lamb to placate the masses so they say now we've done something about it and then we can move on. *Kristy – Social Worker*

Crisis management by dismissal

Thus it seemed inevitable that government response to the media outrage would take the form of government ministers turning ferociously on both the practitioners and the senior managers involved. Haringey Social Services came very quickly under the spotlight. The initial Serious Case Review (SCR) conducted within Haringey Social Services (by the Haringey Local Safeguarding Children Board) in November 2008 was immediately enmeshed in political controversy. The document was placed in the public domain in October 2010 in the interests of 'closure'. While critical of the numerous failures and delays in the handling of the 'Child A' (Baby Peter) case it reads blandly in places. Typical is:

> 1.5.31. There were many factors that contributed to the inability of the agencies to understand what was happening to child A. With the possible exception of the paediatric assessment of 01.08.07, none on their own were likely to have enabled further responses that might have prevented the tragic outcome. The factors in combination contributed to the lack of understanding of the family's functioning and consequently compounded the risk to child A (Department for Education 2010a: 8).

The local MP for Haringey, Lynne Featherstone, who had been a councillor at the time of the Victoria Climbié death, made efforts to have the SCR placed in the public domain. This was resisted by Children's Secretary Ed Balls. Finally Featherstone was able to read the report but under conditions in which she could not reveal its contents. As far as she was concerned the document should have been published as soon as possible. She later commented that, although the report had mentioned numerous failings and lack of co-ordination by agencies,

> this casualness and lack of care is only really demonstrated if you get to read the whole document. It does not come through in the summary and itself is cumulatively causal in my view (Featherstone 2009).

Although the report had been written by an independent author commissioned by Haringey it appeared to Featherstone to have been too amenable to influence by the very senior management whose conduct it was supposed to be evaluating. In this context public scrutiny is an important safeguard:

> Far from being a danger, the light of public scrutiny should be an essential safeguard to ensure that these reviews are carried out properly. Because – quite frankly – these reviews are barely 'independent' as they are commissioned by the Safeguarding Children board – in this case chaired by Sharon Shoesmith, one of the very people whose own actions are up for questioning. The 'independent' person commissioned on this one has already gone public on the fact that he wasn't given any independent access to people or documents and that the report went to the sub-committee (chaired by Ms. Shoesmith) something like five times for 'correction' (Featherstone 2008).

The perception that the SCR was insufficiently independent prompted Ed Balls to commission a second review which was published in March 2009. The second SCR did not mince its words:

> 4.7. Child A's horrifying death could and should have been prevented. If the assumptions and approaches described in this report had been applied...the developments in the case would have been stopped in its tracks at the first serious incident (Department for Education 2010b).

The mistakes included lack of sharing of information between agencies (police, medical and social services) but also the seeming lack of ability of all agencies concerned with Baby Peter to work out what was going on: to establish what was the relationship between Connelly and Barker or what Baby Peter's injuries implied; poor attendance at case conferences and the fact that the designated social worker made ten visits to the family home, the last occurring four days before his death and failing to pick up the risk of death, were also cited as major errors. I shall return to these issues in the next chapter.

However, this second SCR was published in March 2009. Balls had not waited for its publication before dismissing Shoesmith. He had followed the initial SCR by commissioning, under section 20 of the Children Act 2004, a 'Joint Area Review' (JAR) into Haringey by Ofsted, HM Inspectorate of Constabulary and the Health-care Commission. The JAR reported at the end of November 2008 and

> identified a number of serious concerns in relation to safe-guarding of children and young people in Haringey. The con-tribution of local services to improving outcomes for children and young people at risk or requiring safeguarding is inade-quate and needs urgent and sustained attention (Ofsted et al. 2008: 3).

On the basis of this Balls moved to dismiss Shoesmith in early December 2008 and her formal sacking by Haringey followed soon after. The following April Haringey announced the dismissal of four other employees: Clive Preece, head of children in need and safe-guarding services, Cecilia Hitchen, deputy director of children's ser-vices, the team manager of children's services Gillie Christou and Maria Ward who had been Baby Peter's allocated social worker at the time of his murder. All of these, from Shoesmith down, chal-lenged their dismissal through the courts. Of these Shoesmith natu-rally enough received the greatest publicity. Unlike David Scott, the head of London Probation Area a few months later, Shoesmith did not go quietly.

The Ofsted JAR featured heavily in the legal drama. One reason that Balls had commissioned the Ofsted inspection was, it was widely assumed, that a previous Ofsted report, in October 2007, had given Haringey a clean bill of health regarding child protection. Embarrassingly (for Balls) this report had been conducted *after* the death of Baby Peter in August of that year. The report concluded that 'Haringey Borough Council delivers a good service for children and young people' (Ofsted 2007: 1) and that:

> The number of children on the child protection register continues to decrease and is now in line with statistical neighbours. Thorough quality assurance systems are in place and the number of re-registrations demonstrates effective planning for these children (Ofsted 2007: 4).

For this reason alone the latest Ofsted-led JAR was bound to be controversial, especially in its role as the instigator of Shoesmith's dismissal. As the court case proceeded allegations surfaced that this report had been 'beefed up' to put Shoesmith in a bad light. For example the final draft of the report referred to 'insufficient strategic leadership and management oversight' regarding child protection. This phrase was not in the previous draft. However Ofsted responded that such changes were a normal part of the drafting process and Ed Balls added that 'There can be no suggestion but that the JAR was independent and acted at all times as such – no political interference with process, or conclusions, is or could be alleged' (BBC News 2010a).

There is no intention here to comment on the validity or otherwise of the various allegations. The important point is the simple fact that the matter had reached the courts as a result of Shoesmith's dismissal by Balls and, whatever anyone said or did, the matter had become tainted with suggestions of political pressure. A possible consequence of this was underlined by the trial judge in Shoesmith's challenge to her dismissal, Mr Justice Foskett, who, while confirming that Shoesmith had been lawfully dismissed, added that the actions of Haringey in sacking her so rapidly after Balls dismissed her from her post as Director of Children's Services (DCS) did give the appearance of being unfair. He noted that:

> there is the wider concern of who will undertake the role of DCS if someone can be removed in these circumstances without a proper and obviously fair process...That could potentially impact on the whole structure of the child safeguarding arrangements throughout the country, which everyone, whatever their views

about this particular case, must regard as extremely important (see Higgs 2010).

Others echoed these sentiments:

> John Chowcat, general secretary of the children's services union Aspect, said: "This can really worry and demoralise children's services managers, when what we actually need is good senior leaders moving up the profession." Marion Davis, president of the Association of Directors of Children's Services, said DCSs had experienced increasing government scrutiny bordering on "micro-management". She said: "We must not allow raw politics to simplify or distort what are complex and serious matters concerning the safety of children" (see Higgs 2010).

The issue is not that grave mistakes were not made by social workers and their managers regarding Baby Peter. The point is rather the form of the response and the way the case became a politicised and litigious conflict in a manner entirely absent from the Colwell inquiry 30 years previously. The Baby Peter tragedy occurred in the same borough (Haringey) in which Victoria Climbié had died in 2000. Nigel Parton had compared the Colwell and Climbié inquiries:

> the most crucial difference is, perhaps, in relation to the way the inquiry itself operated. A number of witnesses were clearly very reluctant to appear, and in one case the senior social worker was subsequently charged and fined £500 by a court. Numerous papers and files seem to have been destroyed or lost. There were various delays in the proceedings because of the non appearance of files and witnesses, and the inquiry reconvened on two separate occasions as a result. This was in relation not only to a senior social worker involved but also the Chief of the Social Services Inspectorate. At numerous points in the inquiry the report is quite clear that a number of witnesses were at best 'economical with the truth', or were blatantly lying (Parton 2004: 92).

Parton is not sure whether this reflects

> the high anxiety and tensions that are now generated by such public inquiry events...a particular local and pathological set of

relationships in North London at the time, or...the state that child protection and child welfare practice in this country has come to (Parton 2004: 91).

At the end of the day, for many practitioners, even outside child protection, the whole episode of Shoesmith's dismissal left a nasty taste.

> I was curious to find out how much Ed Balls was involved in this [*the Shoesmith case*]...How much was that an independent judicial conclusion to this as opposed to maybe some kind of pressure from the government? There was a lot of interference from the onset by Ed Balls. Whether that was justified or not is debatable but because of that kind of interference it seemed to me that there wouldn't be any other outcome. *Annabel – Probation Officer*

Probation officers might well sympathise since their service had suffered a similar fate at the hands of the Justice Secretary, Jack Straw. Following the Sonnex murders in June 2008 the first step was an internally conducted Serious Further Incident report (roughly the parallel of the SCR in child protection). The initial Serious Further Offence (SFO) was conducted, as would normally be the case, internally by London Probation Area and was completed by September 2008. This, to the amazement of many practitioners, found itself in the public domain:

> Sonnex was interesting because it was the first time that a serious further offence resulted in ministers deciding that they were going to blow Probation's cover. They did that by releasing into the public domain all of the relevant internal reports...The internal report, which up to then had always been understood as being an internal matter...I can remember actually seeing it on the News At Ten...it was there, they had a copy of it, it was on the screen! *Philip – Senior Probation Manager*

Further pressure from various quarters, including the French government (the murders having caused an uproar in France) led to the decision, presumably by Jack Straw, that a further SFO would be conducted by the National Offender Management Service (NOMS). This was completed in January 2009 and was also placed in the public domain (Hill 2009).

The NOMS report refers to two significant errors of judgement and breakdowns in communication. The first concerned the lack of co-ordination between agencies, notably the failure of earlier medical assessment of Sonnex while in prison to be passed on to the probation service. The second concerns incorrect risk assessment – Sonnex was mistakenly assessed as 'medium risk' as a consequence of which he received inadequate supervision. These issues will be discussed in more detail in the next chapter. It should be noted here however that, unlike Haringey child protection, London Probation did not dismiss any practitioners. None were identified as having behaved negligently in the circumstances in which they found themselves.

What is more significant is that the NOMS report, while echoing the themes of the initial SFO and also confirming that shortcomings of practice had been identified and addressed, contained a criticism which is nowhere to be found in the original SFO conducted by London Probation Area (LPA):

> Performance weaknesses took place within the LPA in a context of too little awareness at the most senior levels in the organisation about both locality capacity and competence factors (Hill 2009: 3).

This reference to 'the most senior levels in the organisation' appears in the initial summary at the beginning of the report but does not receive further elaboration in the main body of the report. True, the point is made that a 'key weakness was the limited knowledge "senior managers" appeared to have of "locality capacity and competence factors"' (Hill 2009: 16) but it is immediately added that changes implemented from January 2009 have addressed the issue. The term 'senior managers', of whom there are many in London Probation or any other Probation Area or Trust, is, furthermore, quite different in implication from 'the most senior levels in the organisation' which, intended or not, points to censure of the Chief Officer himself.

The NOMS report was published in January 2009. Shortly afterwards, Scott resigned in a principled manner, taking the responsibility for the failures of his organisation:

> My mantra from day one in London was that the buck stopped with me as Chief Officer (I was advised from above that this was an inherently risky position to take). I resigned as Chief Officer for London Probation because something had gone badly wrong. Two innocent young men had died terrible deaths at the hands of Sonnex and another individual. Failings by the service I led and the wider criminal justice system contributed to their deaths (Scott 2010: 292–293).

The international dimension to the Sonnex case in the form of demands from the French government to know how someone under probation supervision had been able to murder two of its citizens, combined with the fact that the case came so soon after the murders of Naomi Bryant and John Monckton, in both cases by individuals under probation supervision, led to questions in the House of Commons. Straw was called upon to make a statement in which he said: 'As secretary of state responsible for the probation and prison services, I take responsibility for their failings' (quoted in Tran 2009). Of course this might, in an earlier epoch, have led Straw to resign himself. Instead, such old-fashioned integrity was left to David Scott. Straw said:

> I did not consider resigning. I don't think resigning would be an appropriate thing to do. I decided towards the end of last year, when I first became acquainted with the full horrific details not only of the murders – but also what had gone wrong, that it was my duty to set about putting things right (quoted in Travis & Gillan 2009).

'Putting things right' led Straw to threaten Scott with a 'performance capability review' but Straw was denied this little exercise of power by Scott's principled resignation. Straw allegedly claimed that Scott had been suspended and would be sacked when in fact neither had occurred.

Scott's behaviour might be contrasted with Shoesmith's, but that would not add anything in the way of clarification to the problems facing either child protection or probation. Scott did indeed hit back at Straw, albeit from the pages of the practitioner oriented academic publication *Probation Journal:*

> nothing had prepared me for the duplicity of the agency nor, more shockingly, the posturing of the then Justice Secretary in the national media. Why the Justice Secretary should state that I had been suspended when I had not remains a mystery to me. His assertion that I would have been sacked (prejudging any hearing) is deeply ironic coming from the head of the Ministry of Justice. I had expected and received intrusive door-stepping by the media at my home but not careless falsehoods from those with the power to provide perspective and balance. Does this matter, or is it just another symptom of the political life in our country which has descended to such tawdry depths? (Scott 2010: 93).

Scott hit the nail on the head. Political life has indeed declined in quality precisely as government by media has risen to become a major driving force. Practitioners were well aware of this:

> They [*the government*] want to be seen as effective and strong in their interventions by having these kind of hard line 'look at us dealing with this'. Distancing themselves away from any culpability for these things happening rather than looking at why people come to do such horrible things generally through those people's own backgrounds. *Kristy – Social Worker*

> With Sonnex the chief probation officer of London was forced to resign in pretty poor circumstances, it has to be said…It was clear to me at the time, Ministers wanted to be seen to be tough, to be seen to be making decisions and to be seen…this was not their responsibility, they were sorting it out now…its someone else's responsibility…in this case you target the chief officer. *Philip – Senior Probation Manager*

Avoiding the issues – resources

The government's media-driven damage limitation exercise and high profile dismissals and resignations also had the effect of attempting to define the issues, both in child protection and probation, as essentially managerial: matters of the failure of senior management to effectively supervise.

> The stance taken by the Minister...was that...[*the Sonnex case*] ...was essentially a managerial failure that necessitated the resignation of the Chief Officer for the London Probation Area. This suggests a basic lack of understanding of the underlying and sustained difficulties facing the London Probation Area given its size and demographic complexities, severe staff shortages, which in turn were compounded by difficulties in retaining experienced staff, excessive workloads and ineffective information systems. It also suggests a lack of communication between the Secretary of State and his own officials who were encouraging probation areas to under spend in order to cover future redundancies (Burke 2009: 220).

In particular, Straw, despite taking 'full responsibility' explicitly ruled out any connection between failure and lack of resources. In a public statement he claimed:

> Those failures were not a question of poor resources, but of poor judgments and poor management in London Probation, as well as errors by the Metropolitan police and the Prison Service. As Secretary of State responsible for the probation service and the Prison Service, I take responsibility for their failings, and the Metropolitan police take responsibility for their failings. On behalf of each agency, I have apologised to the families of Laurent Bonomo and Gabriel Ferez, and I do so publicly again today....But nor were those failures the result of a lack of resources—probation funding has increased by 70 per cent in real terms since 1997, and London Probation underspent its £154 million budget last year by £3.5 million—rather, this was a failure to use the resources available to London Probation effectively (Hansard 2009).

David Scott openly criticised Straw in the press, arguing that for:

> Jack Straw, the Justice Secretary, to dismiss lack of resources
> as a factor in the Sonnex case and to deny that there is any
> such lack in the service as a whole is quite simply wrong (Scott
> 2009).

Scott explained that the £3.5 million underspend in London and
£17 million nationally cited by Straw is the direct result of a decision by the National Offender Management Service in October 2008
to encourage all probation boards to maximise underspends:

> Financial planning within the Ministry has been so abject that
> it has been impossible to predict what level of expenditure
> probation areas could expect. Therefore money had to be kept
> back so that it could be carried over into the following year's
> budget to meet exigencies, including potential redundancies
> (Scott 2009).

As to the impact this had on the supervision of Dano Sonnex, at the
time he committed his murders Lewisham probation was 'in melt-
down' and severely lacking in resources. Sonnex was supervised by a
probation officer who was inexperienced, and only qualified for
nine-months, with a caseload of 127. Ten years ago the caseload for
such an officer would have been around 30–35. Moreover only one
out of the 22 probation officers in Lewisham had more than two
years' experience. The official inquiry reports into the Sonnex case
noted high sickness rates due to stress and anxiety and missing risk
assessments in 650 of the 2,500 cases supervised by the Lewisham
office (Fitzgibbon 2009). For Straw to argue that this was simply
a bad distribution of resources within London Probation Area
seems disingenuous in the light of David Scott's point about the
necessity of underspend arising from the unpredictability of resource
availability.

There was, of course, more at stake than simply lack of resources.
The whole government strategy of deskilling and outsourcing of
probation services, cost-cutting of front-line services in the face
of inflated bureaucracy (of which more in the following chapter),
provoked David Ramsbotham, former HM Inspector of Prisons, to

defend Scott as having been put in an impossible position. He described:

> trying to come in on budget as trying to land a jumbo on a postage stamp...while he was desperately trying to invest in more staff, he was told that all this was subject to national contracts. And, most telling of all, while a poor, young and inexperienced probation officer was struggling with 127 individual cases, the already grossly inflated NOMS was expanding its staff to number 4270...If Jack Straw and Phil Wheatley [*head of NOMS*] do not resign, they should also be subject to a performance capability review for what the Sonnex verdict exposes of the damage they have done to the probation service (Ramsbotham 2009).

In child protection the situation has been similar but also with some key differences. At the time of the death of Baby Peter Haringey social workers were overloaded. Maria Ward, the social worker assigned to Baby Peter, was the allocated social worker for 18 different cases despite the Haringey recommendation of a maximum of 12. This was in fact a repeat of the situation at the time of the Victoria Climbié case in which the allocated social worker, Lisa Arthur-worrey, was dismissed and barred from further social work. This was later rescinded after a ruling on appeal that she had been well overstretched with 19 cases.

However, the blaze of publicity in which child protection social work found itself following Baby Peter, enhanced by Shoesmith's very public challenge to her dismissal and by the fact that a high profile public inquiry under the chairmanship of Lord Laming had reported only five years previously on Haringey's handling of the Victoria Climbié case in 2000, meant that things took a different turn regarding resources. Ed Balls, rather than stonewalling in the manner of Jack Straw, called Laming back to do a second report on child protection. This had two consequences.

First, it provided an opportunity for the trade union Unison to voice the concerns of its social work members on issues such as resources and workloads by submitting evidence to Lord Laming. Unison conducted a survey for this purpose and found that 43 percent of respondents agreed that 'systems and procedures' and inter-agency working had improved since 2003, the year of the first Laming

Report into the Victoria Climbié case but 49 percent thought that social work was worse off in terms of resources than in 2003. Only nine percent thought that things had actually improved. Meanwhile nearly 60 percent of respondents were working in teams where over 20 percent of posts remained vacant. Nearly three quarters of all respondents (71%) saw average caseloads as having increased since 2003. Finally, almost two thirds (60%) of respondents said that non-qualified social work staff were more likely to be doing child protection work than in 2003 (UNISON 2008). Had a similar public inquiry taken place into the state of probation services it would have been interesting to speculate on what the responses to a similar survey of members conducted by the National Association of Probation Officers might have been. The more secretive and 'in-house' inquiries following the Sonnex case however meant that such opportunities did not become available.

The second effect of Laming was that government had to make a public response to the issues raised and resource commitments could hardly be avoided. Consequently, as part of the Department for Children, Schools and Families' response, Ed Balls announced an allocation of £57.8 million for new social work training. Such recognition of the needs of social work training is obviously to be welcomed but for some hard-working practitioners the damage had already been done:

> damaging the very service that needs to be strengthened in order to protect children...I'm sorry Ed Balls, its a witch-hunt and then 'oh we really need good social workers'. You've just given the population of Britain every reason why they would never want to be a social worker. Every social worker I speak to now has this terrible fear that one day their face will be on the front page of the paper saying they practically killed a child. *Kristy – Social Worker*

> At the same time as Baby P. you have the Labour government providing Surestart, looking at interventions and attempting to go in the right direction. At the same time they are blaming/ destroying the support staff group that enables those initiatives to work. *Pippa – Social Work Manager*

There is indeed little to suggest, at least under the previous New Labour government, anything resembling a fundamental critique and appraisal of methods of work in either social services or probation. While cases like Baby Peter and Sonnex are mercifully rare, when things do go wrong they shine a light on the working of the system and an opportunity for reform.

Avoiding the issues – working methods

Laming and child protection

The Laming Inquiry of 2003 (Laming 2003) into the death of Victoria Climbié is the nearest that child protection came to anything resembling the Maria Colwell inquiry of 1974. A key difference was that Laming was not a public inquiry, which meant that important people like neighbours and Victoria's parents were not given a chance to speak. Nevertheless, as Parton (2004) has commented, many of Laming's conclusions, particularly those relating to the failure of agencies to communicate and of social workers to miss key symptoms of abuse, had a familiar ring. Laming was high profile and wide ranging, unlike the more restricted and 'in-house' investigations following the Sonnex and similar preceding cases.

However, despite consulting widely among professionals involved in various aspects of child protection, Laming's perspective was restricted: his task was basically to patch up the system and show it could be reformed without too much restructuring and fundamental rethinking about the working methods of social workers. His report(s) confirm the notion that the 'task of inquiries into particular crises is to represent failure as temporary, or no failure at all, and to re-establish the image of administrative and legal coherence and rationality' (Burton & Carlen 1979: 48).

This is reflected strongly in the powerful theme of surprise that runs through the report, as if he was asking in a rather perplexed way, 'Why aren't you (the agencies concerned with child protection) doing what you are supposed to?' Thus one of his themes was the failure of communication between different agencies. This of course had been an issue at the time of Colwell. Laming simply tells the police, for example, that they had better devote more resources to the issue and regard child protection as a priority. Thus:

> Chief constables must ensure that crimes involving a child victim are dealt with promptly and efficiently, and to the same standard as equivalent crimes against adults. (recommendation 92) [*and*

that] officers working on child protection teams are sufficiently well trained in criminal investigation, and that there is always a substantial core of fully trained detective officers on each team to deal with the most serious inquiries (recommendation 97) (Laming 2003: 381).

This, it might be thought, is what the police and social services should have been doing anyway. However, as Judith Masson (2006) observes, Laming failed to grasp the work of the police as an agency against the backdrop of the constraints imposed by Home Office targets and priorities. The focus on maximisation of sanction detections, although the subject of its own debates and criticisms (see Fitzgibbon & Lea 2010), acts as a constraint on resources available to police investigation of child abuse.

Whilst policing is seen in terms of the efficiency of investigations or the reduction of crime, it should not be surprising that police work relating to all but the most serious crimes within families is given a low priority. This should not be viewed as the perverse response of Chief Constables but the logical consequence of the leadership they have had from central government (Masson 2006: 235).

This is perhaps slightly unfair in that Laming did pick up in one of his discussions the conclusion that:

As regards child protection, it was said that until the protection of children features in the Home Secretary's 'Police Priorities' list, it was unlikely that steps would necessarily be taken at a local level to improve the quality of police child protection teams (Laming 2003: 358).

Doing something about this would have involved Laming's taking a holistic 'big picture' perspective but he was necessarily focused on 'local failings'. As Masson commented:

it is to be expected that an inquiry established by ministers will focus on finding local failings. A detailed analysis of what happened is necessary to determine who did (or omitted to do) what, and to allocate blame. This cannot be seen as an objective process if central government and some parties, like Victoria's parents, are shielded from the spotlight of potential responsibility. The broader questions why the system operated in the way it did and how this might be addressed require more attention to be given to the bigger picture. What are the current problems facing agencies with child protection responsibilities? And what is the impact of legislation, policy, target setting, and monitoring on their practices? (Masson 2006: 242).

A second 'local failing' which surprised Laming was the failure of communication between managers and front-line social workers. He reports that:

A succession of senior managers and councillors from Haringey gave evidence before me and expressed their complete surprise at the state of the council's front-line services as revealed by the evidence given to this Inquiry by social workers and their immediate managers. It is the job of the leaders of any organisation to be aware of conditions on the 'shop floor' and the standard of service provided to its customers. It is their job to identify deficiencies in that service and put them right. Ignorance cannot, in my view, be a legitimate defence (Laming 2003: 197–198).

I have already noted that this was one of the themes that cropped up in the January 2009 NOMS report on handling of the Sonnex case by London Probation. I shall return to this presently. Parton (2004) identified this as a key difference from the situation at the time of Colwell. Then the key issue had been the relations between case workers; by the time of Climbié it was:

much more in relation to wide-ranging and complex system failures, of which communication between individual workers is simply a part. This is a consequence not only of the growth of a variety of new procedures which has taken place over the intervening thirty years, but also the growth in use of information technology of one sort or another for a variety of purposes. The failures were not so much in sharing information but managing information, and it is in this respect that the notion of 'systematic care' is seen as so important for ensuring that information and knowledge are managed rigorously, and where there are clear lines of accountability and responsibility (Parton 2004: 88).

It is nevertheless extraordinary that so many of Laming's recommendations to senior managers amount to little more than 'do your job', with reminders to ensure that social workers are properly trained for the particular job they are undertaking (recommendation 43), that they understand their job (recommendation 46), that files must be properly read and reviewed (recommendation 49) and that strategy meetings result in a list of action points being drawn up and circulated to all concerned (recommendation 51).

The theme of practitioners failing to do what they were supposed to do is at its strongest when it comes to the social workers directly concerned with Victoria Climbié: that over a period of 211 days Victoria was only seen on four occasions by her designated social worker, that these visits were never longer than 30 minutes, that conversation with Victoria was minimal and the total time spent by the social worker spent discussing Victoria's case with others responsible for supervising her work was no more than 30 minutes in total (Laming 2003: 196). Laming gives the impression of exasperation when he prefaces his recommendations with the remark that:

some of what follows may be thought by some to be self-evident or to amount to little more than a call for social workers to do the job they have been trained to do and are paid to carry out. I have some sympathy with this sentiment, as I was often struck during the course of the evidence to this inquiry by the basic nature of the failures illustrated by Victoria's case (Laming 2003: 196).

This is certainly the impression created by the fact that Laming should have to remind social workers that they:

must not undertake home visits without being clear about the purpose of the visit, the information to be gathered during the course of it, and the steps to be taken if no one is at home. No visits should be undertaken without the social worker concerned checking the information known about the child by other child protection agencies. All visits must be written up on the case file (recommendation 34).

While social workers needed better training, senior managers needed better accountability. 'Never again should people in senior positions be free to claim – as they did in this inquiry – ignorance of what was happening to children' (Laming 2003: 8). This implied clear lines of accountability and of course clear record keeping. Clear record keeping was central also to the problem of interagency co-ordination. Laming saw it as essential that there should be a centralised database rather than different agencies having different bits of information without a guarantee that anyone would see the whole picture (recommendation 12). This was one of the things that had gone wrong in the treatment of Victoria Climbié in which, due to her immigrant status, different agencies at times failed to realise they were dealing with the same child (Masson 2006).

A further key recommendation was for the abolition of the Child Protection Register. Laming had recommended this on the grounds that staff felt under pressure to reduce the number of children on the register with the added 'danger that other agencies may make unwarranted assumptions of the level of help and support being given to a child whose name is on the register' (Laming 2003: 366). Rather there should be a 'National Children's Database on all children under the age of 16' (recommendation 17) under the auspices of a National Agency for Children and Families. In other words, rather than starting from those children found to be at risk, Laming advocated a preventative approach which started with the surveillance of all children.

A number of observers have pointed to the limitations of Laming's approach which, as we have seen, was to a considerable extent dictated by the type of inquiry he was tasked by government to undertake. The most trenchant criticism is that Laming in 2003 gave a detailed account of the failures in the Victoria Climbié case but little in the way of analysis of why it happened. Thus Laming:

> begins with an impassioned and wide-ranging series of reflections, analyses, and judgements, but it ends much as most inquiry reports have, by resort to a combination of recommendations for structural

change and tightening of procedures. In between are the lengthy narrative reconstructions of contact between the various services, Victoria herself, and those who were supposed to be caring for her. Through these stories we see that people repeatedly failed to come to grips professionally with the evidence that was presented to them. But we do not see why and how this happened (Cooper et al. 2003: 25).

Eileen Munro, writing after the return of Laming to chair the second inquiry following the death of Baby Peter, is even more hard-hitting:

Since most [*social workers*] do not intend to make mistakes, when we find them doing so we should not just criticise them and order them to do better; we need to look further to see why their misguided action looked reasonable to them at the time.

Lord Laming's 2003 report into the care provided to Victoria Climbié signally failed to do this, providing a detailed account of what went wrong but no understanding of why it happened. He concluded his inquiry by expressing amazement that so many professionals failed to do basic things properly. He appears to be equally unable to understand what is happening now, instead telling people to improve and expressing his frustration in capital letters: 'NOW JUST DO IT'.

It is reasonable to assume that those who have chosen to dedicate their careers to helping children are at least as concerned as Lord Laming about improving their safety and welfare. Therefore, the dysfunctional picture of practice painted by the report is deeply puzzling and merits closer scrutiny. Why have the well-intentioned reforms, implemented by well-intentioned people, led to such disarray? Lord Laming's progress report fails to give an answer. It primarily offers a description of what has happened in children's services in recent years but lacks any analysis of why matters have evolved in so many dysfunctional ways (Munro 2009).

The basic criticism here is that Laming missed an opportunity, rather than telling everyone to do what they were supposed to do, to take a fundamental look at how the whole orientation to targets and the orientation to risk management was having damaging effects on the relationship between social workers and clients: to, in Munro's terms, try and find out why it was that social workers made fundamental mistakes.

The rolling out of the national children's database (known as Contact-Point) and a new centralised computer record keeping system under the title of Integrated Children's System (ICS) would take practitioners even further away from the front-line. The New Labour government responded to Laming with the 2003 Green Paper *Every Child Matters* (Chief Secretary to the Treasury 2003), and the Children's Act 2004. The child protection register was to be phased out by 2008 and replaced by child protection plans for those seen as vulnerable. Meanwhile the 2004 Act produced a new bureaucracy of a Children's Commissioner for England and Local Safeguarding Children Boards with a general theme of inter-agency co-operation to secure the well-being of all children which included physical and mental health and emotional well-being, protection from harm and neglect, education, training and recreation, the contribution made by them to society, and social and economic well-being.

Laming appeared to have attempted to solve some problems by intensifying others. Two main criticisms developed: first, that the new ICS recording system was increasing the pressure on practitioners to spend less time with clients. On the day Laming's second report into Baby Peter was published, Eileen Munro said:

> in eight months nobody had a significant conversation with Victoria...and yet now, social workers are spending 80 percent of their time in front of a computer so they hardly have time to speak to the parents let alone to the children (BBC Today 2009).

Secondly, critics argue that the abolition of the child protection register in favour of a preventative approach which starts from the lives of all children is actually making abused children more, rather than less vulnerable. Thus although the different agencies working with children (education, police, health, social services) are supposed to develop better co-ordination, where 'protection from harm and neglect' is buried among the several other priorities listed above, child abuse can easily drop through the middle. The National Society for the Prevention of Cruelty to Children (NSPCC), the leading voluntary sector body in child protection, made a similar point in its evidence to Laming's second, 2009, inquiry. While welcoming the impetus for greater interagency collaboration in child protection deriving from *Every Child Matters* the NSPCC warned that:

> We believe it is possible that the current emphasis on the broad safeguarding agenda, with its emphasis on prevention and early intervention, could inadvertently have had the consequence of reducing the focus on protecting the most vulnerable children. We think it is also possible that the emphasis on supporting vulnerable parents might inadvertently have had the consequence of reducing the centrality of the vulnerable child (NSPCC 2008b: 2).

Davies & Duckett (2008) combine both criticisms:

> If Victoria Climbié 's name had been on the register she would have had a child protection plan to keep her safe, hospitals and police would have been alerted to the risks, professionals would have followed her care from borough to borough and the case would have been analysed in a multi-agency setting. Yet surprisingly, Lord Laming recommended the abolition of the register.
>
> ...There is no replacement for the register although there is now provision for a child to be designated as the subject of a child protection plan. A children's database for every child in the country now named ContactPoint...represents an unprecedented and unwarranted invasion of children's and families' privacy. Professionals overwhelmed with meeting performance targets, responding to low level concerns, preoccupied with data entry, and under pressure to close cases within predefined timescales for assessments, find it difficult to focus their attention on children at risk of harm. Research by the University of York confirmed that social workers found the ICS forms too prescriptive, repetitive and time-consuming and that the tick boxes were often irrelevant or too imprecise to be useful. The forms were unwieldy and not fit for use as court reports or reports for conferences. On average it took 8.5 hours to complete a core assessment and 2.5 hours for initial assessments (Davies & Duckett 2008: 15).

Such an approach can be positive only if the social workers who are making the interventions are well trained and sensitive to the dangers of labelling children at an early stage with detrimental effects to both the child and his or her family. Such a holistic, early intervention approach aimed at children in general could, in the hands of inexperienced or unqualified practitioners, additionally do considerable damage since early labelling and adverse assessments could impact upon children in a very similar way to the effect of adverse risk assessments on offenders during the early stage of their offending history.

Space prevents a discussion of the more general issues of surveillance and privacy (but see Penna 2005; Wrennall 2010). Attention must turn to the calling back of Laming to produce a second report in 2009 following the death of Baby Peter. Laming's ostensible brief was to:

> evaluate the good practice that has been developed since the publication of the report of the Independent Statutory Inquiry following the death of Victoria Climbié, to identify the barriers that are now preventing good practice becoming standard practice, and recommend actions to be taken to make systematic improvements in safeguarding children across the country (Laming 2009: 3).

In fact the frustration identified by Munro often comes to the surface. The fact that good practice has not yet become standard practice despite the recommendations, policy and subsequent legislation (see below) arising from his previous report leaves Laming at a loss:

> The utility of the policy and legislation has been pressed on me by contributors throughout this report. In such circumstances it is hard to resist the urge to respond by saying to each of the key services, if that is so "NOW JUST DO IT!" (Laming 2009: 6–7).

His identification of the barriers to the progress that ought to have followed from his earlier recommendations amounts to the usual suspects: staff time, knowledge and skills (para. 1.5), significant problems with inter-agency co-ordination and information sharing (para. 1.6) and low quality of training and heavy case-loads for front line staff (para. 1.7). He concludes that:

> To effect a step change in services and to transform outcomes for children and young people the priority given to safeguarding must be achieved through strong and effective leadership, early

intervention, adequate resources, and quality performance management, inspection and support (Laming 2009: 13).

Some of his recommendations seem to simply repeat those from his earlier report:

> The Home Secretary and the Secretaries of State for Children, Schools and Families, Health, and Justice must collaborate in the setting of explicit strategic priorities for the protection of children and young people and reflect these in the priorities of frontline services (Laming 2009: 15).

Haven't we just been reading this? In his 2003 report he had already said that:

> there would be considerable benefit to be gained from all the services knowing their local communities better and by services being more accessible to the communities they serve. Key services could do this directly themselves or involve community-based organisations, such as voluntary and charitable organisations. Each local authority needs to develop a strategy to achieve this and to ensure that it happens in practice (Laming 2003: 352).

There is a difference in emphasis in the reports between local and national but the message is essentially the same: co-ordinate resources to deliver effective child protection. As with the previous report, there is no hint of a challenge to the existing ways of working but rather a call for yet more targets and performance indicators: the government should 'introduce new statutory targets for safeguarding and child protection' (Laming 2009: 16). The report continues, making various recommendations that, even if not in precise formulation, at least in spirit, *have already been said in the previous report.*

> Directors of Children's Services, Chief Executives of Primary Care Trusts, Police Area Commanders and other senior service managers must regularly review all points of referral where concerns about a child's safety are received to ensure they are sound in terms

of the quality of risk assessments, decision making, onward referrals
and multi-agency working (Laming 2009: 19).

Other recommendations have an unworldly ring to them. Munro,
again, is highly critical:

> When you look closely at the list of 58 recommendations, it reads
> more like a wish list for Santa Claus than a feasible set of actions.
> Number 55, for example, says there must be sufficient resources
> to ensure that early intervention and preventative services have
> capacity to respond to all children and families identified as vul-
> nerable or 'in need'—a number estimated by the government to
> be 3–4 million children per year (Munro 2009).

There was, though, one important substantive recommendation which
led to government action. This was the commitment of £57.8 million
for improved social work education and recruitment mentioned above.
Whether such a commitment will survive the intentions of the new
coalition government resulting from the May 2010 election to cut
£670 million from children's services (Garboden 2010) is in question.
Cuts will also impact on other elements already in place as a result of
Laming's recommendations such as the early intervention strategy
derived from *Every Child Matters*. As a social worker otherwise in favour
of the early intervention strategy put it:

> early intervention is a good thing, in properly resourced ser-
> vices. However I am very scared what will happen to these
> early intervention teams with the current economic crisis and
> social services cuts. Already in my borough there has been a
> 50% reduction in the managers of teams, called locality teams,
> who undertake this early interventions work. *Beth – Social Worker*

However the whole strategy may be short lived in view of other
elements of the approach of the new government, notably the decision not to proceed with the national database. The ContactPoint
website now contains the terse statement: 'Ministers do not believe
that a database, which holds details of all children in England and
which is accessible to hundreds of thousands of people, is the right
way to help vulnerable children' (Department for Children 2010).

Laming has been dwelled on in some detail both because of his profile and influence and also because his report and recommendations illustrate the problem of attempting to respond to practitioner failure in the Victoria Climbié and Baby Peter cases without confronting the fundamental methods of work in social services – that is, without 'a rigorous exploration of why people *[i.e. practitioners]* act as they do' (Munro 2009). Meanwhile in the lower profile less publicly visible world of probation remarkably similar issues have emerged as a result of the Sonnex case.

Probation and offender management

Similar issues of responding to problems by tweaking existing procedures and methods of work while failing to look into underlying problems, characterised the response to Sonnex by London Probation. Here there was no Laming; the conditions were different. Scott went quietly of his own accord and no practitioners or managers were suspended as nobody could, despite mistakes having been made, be accused of negligence. The mistakes that were made were remarkably similar to those in child protection: failures of collaboration between agencies (in this case the prison service, police and probation) and mistaken risk assessments by practitioners leading to inadequate supervision of Sonnex.

Both the original SFO report and the NOMS report of January 2009 had identified key issues: Sonnex had been identified as low risk on the day to day Delius tracking system in use at London Probation. This reflected the fact that he turned up on time for interview and was polite and tidy. However he had been assessed as high risk on the Offender Assessment System (OASys) risk assessment system (see next chapter) which is normally reviewed every four months. The waters had been muddied by misleading information about Sonnex's risk level (his behaviour appeared to be improving) being passed by prison to probation on his release. The discrepancies in risk assessment were noticed when Sonnex was referred to the local Multi-Agency Public Protection Arrangements (MAPPA) panel but they were not acted upon, with the result that Sonnex was not placed in approved premises (rather than allowed to go home) as the more serious risk assessment may require. When the mistake had been realised, and indeed Sonnex had committed further offences, there had been mix-ups at court and police had crucially delayed in apprehending him for a return to custody.

The January 2009 NOMS report (Hill 2009) makes the familiar recommendations to tighten up procedures by ensuring:

> that information relevant to the risk posed by a prisoner on release...should be shared with and used by staff responsible for the management of that offender throughout the course of his or her sentence [*and that*] risks presented by higher risk offenders under supervision are being properly prioritised and managed to deliver as safe a level of public protection as is feasible (Hill 2009: 4–5).

We are back again in the familiar territory of reminding managers and practitioners to do what they are supposed to do anyway. Once again, there is no analysis, apart from the usual passing reference to heavy caseloads and stress, of why they should not have done this. If, on the other hand, it is acknowledged that mistakes do happen, then no amount of injunctions and organisational tweaking will prevent them.

Indeed, most of the issues had been raised in the same form a few years previously. Just as Baby Peter was preceded by Victoria Climbié so was Sonnex preceded by Damien Hanson and Elliot White who murdered John Monckton in 2005 and Anthony Rice who murdered Naomi Bryant in 2006. All these individuals were under probation supervision, having been released from prison on licence, when they committed their crimes. In both cases the normal internal SFO reports were succeeded by investigations from HM Inspectorate of Probation – much like an Ofsted inspection in child protection. Both pointed to familiar issues of lack of information flow from the prison authorities to the probation service on release of the offender, sporadic contact with probation supervisors, incorrect risk assessments and management and poor liaison between offender managers and administrators (see HM Inspectorate of Probation 2006a; HM Inspectorate of Probation 2006b).

Rice came very soon after Hanson and White thereby provoking HM Inspectorate of Probation to conduct a more general Thematic Inspection Report on the state of risk management (HM Inspectorate of Probation 2006c). This, again, predictably demanded that:

> High-quality OASys Risk of Harm assessments are completed and used in every case as a key ingredient in effective offender management at all stages of the criminal justice process, and are given a higher profile in prisons...[*and that*]...Information sharing and good recording form the bedrock of effective offender

management at all stages of a sentence, including regular reviews of Risk of Harm (HM Inspectorate of Probation 2006c: 8).

A few years later Dano Sonnex committed his murders and, because he came so soon after Hanson and White and Rice, the NOMS further SFO report of January 2009 (Hill 2009) called for an independent examination of a quarter of the Boroughs – including Lewisham – in which London Probation were responsible for offender supervision. The result was a further HM Inspectorate of Probation report into the management of high risk offenders (HM Inspectorate of Probation 2009). The investigation looked at 276 cases of high risk individuals on community sentences, parole licence and custody. Many practitioners had high caseloads, some senior managers had insufficient experience, there were some examples of good work but in other cases inadequate active management of offenders; reviews of sentence plans were late or simply duplicated original assessments and contained inadequate reviews of risk of harm to the public. The recommendations follow predictably:

> London Probation Area should develop and implement a plan to ensure that, in a higher proportion of cases the overall assessment and management of offenders Risk of Harm to others is of sufficient quality (HM Inspectorate of Probation 2009: 10).

There are obvious parallels with child protection: social workers not meeting with clients or not keeping records and files up to date. Across the two services, child protection and offender management, one gets, having waded through the mountain of reports discussed in this chapter, the strong impression of going round in circles, of unearthing the same problems and repeating endlessly the same recommendations. Laming's frustrated call to 'NOW JUST DO IT' rings in one's ears. Perhaps it is time to respond to Eileen Munro's call for 'a rigorous exploration of why people act as they do' (Munro 2009).

5

The Demise of Probation and Social Service Practice

The last chapter concluded with Eileen Munro's plea for 'a rigorous exploration of why people act as they do' (Munro 2009). Without this we are unable to say whether individual practitioners make the sorts of mistakes that were made in the Sonnex and Baby Peter cases because the existing procedures are too lax or not comprehensively enforced – which has tended to be the assumption – or whether in fact it is the procedures themselves that make it more likely that mistakes will happen because of the way they constrain practitioners to act.

The issue of resources is obviously central to any discussion of why people act as they do. Inexperienced practitioners with absurdly high caseloads are bound to make mistakes because they have insufficient time to check their information, to re-think the problem of what is really going on in a particular case.

> I'm allocating cases to probation officers who are already over-worked...and have been for years. As a manager it makes me feel useless, unable to do anything because these cases have to be allocated out because they are the high-risk cases. I'm unable to do anything about the situation and there is a lack of support from senior managers as to what we can do about that. Of course this is likely to lead to more SFOs [Serious Further Offences] because probation staff cannot manage their work effectively.
> *Charlie – Probation Manager*

Having the time to get to know Dano Sonnex as an individual and the networks within which he moved might have enabled an experienced officer to anticipate that something was likely to go wrong. In fact what resulted was tick-box risk assessments which may or may not have sounded the right warnings but were in any case only picked up, and too late in the day, because they conflicted. Having the time to think through the context in which Baby Peter was suffering his various injuries, what the actual relationship between Connelly and Barker was and how likely it was that they were deploying sophisticated concealment tactics, might have enabled an experienced social worker to see the need for a further visit and a good look round... and thus avoided a child's death. It is obvious that the practitioners involved had neither the time nor the experience to do these things. Add to this the dearth of local surveillance by neighbours and the wider community in such deprived settings and we can understand with hindsight that these were disasters waiting to happen.

But the most important fact about overwork and high caseloads is not the actual work with offenders but, on the contrary, the lack of time to devote to such face to face work.

> I don't think much has improved *[for practitioners]*. The amount of stress on my staff, the amount of burn out, the demands, the amount of time available to work directly with the offenders, I think those are negative changes. They make for a less satisfying job; a more stressful job. *Morgan – Probation Manager*

The new structures of management and bureaucratic accountability imposed by the risk agenda not only reduce time available for face-to-face work with offenders but also increase

> the distance between managers and front-line workers with managers involved in bureaucratic monitoring and control of the administration systems and having little idea of the stressful difficulties faced by practitioners (Collins et al. 2009: 240).

Social workers are also told that technology streamlines and reduces workloads but they reject this claim as their experience indicates the opposite. Participants in the study by Burton and van den Broek (2009: 1339) felt that computer information systems had intensified work and increased requests for information which reduced time available for direct face-to-face work with clients.

The question of time and resources feeds into a second key issue. From Colwell and Young to Sonnex and Baby Peter a key dimension of failure has been the lack of co-ordination and information sharing between agencies: probation, social services, police, medical services and, in the case of offenders, often the prison service. Co-ordination and sharing is absolutely crucial to the management of problematic families and individuals. Different agencies have different skills, work in different ways, are equipped with different statutory powers and collect different types of information. They necessarily remain separate but this makes inter-agency collaboration all the more important. At the same time collaboration with another agency is always an 'extra' task, in addition to the requirements of one's own agency. If agencies are suffering high workloads and are starved of resources then one of the first things to suffer will be collaboration and information sharing with other agencies.

This in turn links to the third issue: the type and quality of the information being shared. Assuming the practitioners of each agency follow their own procedures, the question arises whether the information generated is of such a quality that, when shared with collaborating agencies, it increases knowledge and enables practitioners to take informed action. The key debate here concerns the nature of the various 'tick-box' pre-formatted, computerised templates for risk assessment such as the Offender Assessment System (OASys) used in probation and the Integrated Children's System (ICS) currently deployed in child protection. These systems collect data of a particular type and the issue is whether the latter helps or impedes practitioners in the making of judgements about what is happening and likely to happen in a particular case. Finally, issues arise regarding the nature of information gathered by current techniques and of time and resources available to practitioners to interact. It may be for example that any realistic use of techniques such as OASys, particularly in the case of high-risk serious offenders, requires more time and a reasonable caseload. In this chapter I shall explore some of these interconnections in hope of throwing some light on the real problems facing child protection and the management of serious offenders.

Sharing information

The lack of information sharing between agencies at the time of the Maria Colwell case was, as Butler and Drakeford (2010) point out, to some extent due to the fact that the early 1970s was a period in which different agencies were still fighting it out to establish who was the lead agency in such cases as child death;

> Thus, failure to share information with others in the Colwell case was, to a traceable extent, the result not of incompetence or active disinclination, but of a positive sense of having taken charge of the task with which individuals and agencies had been entrusted (Drakeford & Butler 2010: 1423).

In the Graham Young case, apart from simple mistakes such as the failure of the supervising probation officer to make a home visit – where Young's continued obsession with poisoning might have become evident – there was a simple lack of co-ordination in which those supervising Young on his release were not informed about his history of poisoning. This, as suggested earlier, was partly the product of a different political ethos at the time: that rehabilitation required an ex-offender to start afresh without the burden of his history following him around. The fact, however, that public protection is today the prime consideration and that multi-agency collaboration has become institutionalised and formalised does not seem to have prevented exactly the same issues emerging in the recent cases.

Probation and MAPPA

In criminal justice, multi-agency co-operation has been described as the 'biggest departure in British criminal justice strategy in the past 100 years' (Nash & Williams 2008: 104). In probation, the main formalisation has been the Multi-Agency Public Protection Arrangements (MAPPA) established under the Criminal Justice and Courts' Services Act 2000 which began in each Probation Area or Trust in 2001. The agencies involved include police, probation, and local authority provisions i.e. social services, housing, education, youth services and environmental agencies, as well as voluntary and business organisations. The MAPPA systems works on tiering the offenders into levels of risk. Lowest risk (level one) offenders are managed by a single agency which is usually probation but may also be police or the youth service; higher risk (level two) offenders are managed by

Multi-Agency Risk Management Meetings of staff from various agencies including probation and police, while highest risk (level three) offenders are managed by Multi Agency Public Protection Panels, chaired by a Chief Officer from probation part of whose task is to draw up comprehensive risk management plans and to monitor other agencies involved in the plans. There is a tendency to prioritise public protection and 'containment' over considerations of rehabilitation (Wood & Kemshall 2007). Running parallel to MAPPA are Multi-Agency Risk Assessment Conferences (MARAC) which involve police, probation, prison services, local authority and health agencies liaising to focus on victims through safety plans for individuals at high risk of domestic violence.

Until the establishment of these organisational frameworks interagency collaboration was informal and voluntary and depended very much on the expertise and commitment of the individual practitioners involved. There was often a very high level of commitment. A Retired Chief Probation Officer wrote to the author:

> In the 1970s I was an Assistant Chief Probation Officer...there was one memorable occasion, on a Good Friday afternoon when one of my officers received a telephone call from the estranged and anxious wife of a life-licensee whom she had spotted sitting in a car close to her home, wearing a balaclava and gloves and generally behaving in a suspicious if not threatening manner. The Probation officer promptly phoned me, I contacted a duty officer at the Home Office, who, it being a warm, spring holiday, extricated an under-secretary from his garden! Authority was quickly conveyed to the Kent Police, and the man in question was arrested before he got out of his car!

But the more general issue is how far the more formalised procedures have made a difference or rather the extent to which they ultimately rely on the same commitment that facilitated the informal arrangements.

> It is a very different world between the early 70s and now. In the 70s there would be informal alliances between agencies, you would get excellent work and excellent communication but that was down to individuals. It probably wasn't transferable between

one individual and another. Now we have much more structured our expectations...We've created structure and process, I think we've done a lot of work on understanding, organisationally the need and benefits of working together, of joined up planning, but when you go into any homicide case within health, a child death or SFO we are still looking at failure to properly assess, failure to collect information, failing to consider risks, failing to record information, failing to communicate opinions assessments whatever. We haven't moved an inch. *Morgan – Probation Manager*

When things go wrong it's often because individuals, working under pressure of time and resource constraints, often lacking experience and back-up, make mistakes. This was clear in the Sonnex case. The first thing that went wrong was the failure of information to be communicated from one agency to another as Sonnex passed through the prison system to his eventual release. In May 2004 the doctor in the Aylesbury Young Offender Institution (YOI) had written in his records that 'The forensic dimension is the greatest concern, especially as he admits that his reactions could kill' (see Hill 2009: 8). This information had got lost in Sonnex's transfer from YOI to adult prison and it was not allowed to balance the fact that his behaviour in prison had improved considerably when he stopped taking drugs. Here, it would seem, was an obvious failing amenable to remedy by tightening the procedures. Just make sure that 'information relevant to the risk posed by a prisoner on release, no matter where such information originates from, should be shared with and used by staff responsible for the management of that offender throughout the course of his or her sentence' (Hill 2009: 9). Of course none of this will prevent over-worked practitioners losing files or simply forgetting to pass information on where no one agency is responsible for monitoring an offender such as Sonnex throughout the length of his sentence from YOI through to release on licence.

As we have seen, key mistakes already were made in the Sonnex case in areas that were almost picked up by MAPPA. By the time Sonnex was released, his risk assessment by the prison authorities assessed him as medium risk (the problems with the system of risk assessments will be discussed presently) and as noted above, this largely seemed to result from his improved behaviour on transfer to adult prison and cessation of drug taking (the medical notes having been seemingly forgotten). Before that, while he was taking drugs, he was assessed as high risk but it was the medium risk assessment that was passed on to his probation supervising team on release.

The supervising probation officer was concerned about Sonnex receiving only a medium risk assessment – as soon as he was released he started committing offences again including threatening people, so she referred the case to MAPPA. But the referral to MAPPA was delayed by a combination of administrative incompetence and failure to see the urgency of reclassification of Sonnex's risk level. There had indeed been some new events which ought to have changed his risk level and which MAPPA should have considered: Sonnex made violent threats to a pregnant woman and her partner to extort money but this did not lead to a criminal conviction due to the charges being dropped and so was not included in a new risk evaluation. This dropping of charges was later found to be due to victim intimidation by Sonnex. When he was finally recalled to prison police incompetence delayed the execution of the warrant. If that hadn't happened then the murders might have been avoided.

It was an individual who picked up the fact that there was something wrong with Sonnex's risk assessment: that either the original assessments were wrong or that his behaviour had moved in a new direction. The real issue is the skills, time and resources at the disposal of such individuals. When MAPPA systems do work it is these factors, rather than the procedures themselves that account for success: exactly the same factors, in other words, that accounted for the success of the old informal procedures.

Indeed, a number of institutional factors are pushing in the opposite direction making interagency collaboration harder, despite formal structures such as MAPPA. First, on a general level reorganisation which integrated probation with the prison service as part of the National Offender Management Service (NOMS) aiming at a seamless web of offender management – a political decision inspired by New Labour's 'rebalancing' the criminal justice system towards an increased emphasis on public protection – has undermined local area links with social services and other agencies which would enable better surveillance and understanding of clients:

> I could not tell you how many restructurings I have been through in London. There were times when probation stayed pretty stable,

and then we learned the game of restructuring, it's impossible. We had a network of multi-agency groups coming together in the London area to begin to work better, sharing information on people with mental health difficulties locally, and in one fell swoop we wiped those out just by restructuring organisations, moving people, and then there was no one in the area who could relate to anyone else over that length of time. I don't want to appear a dinosaur, if there's one thing I've learned it's how to cope with change. Managing change is what I do and why I'm still here. I think change is good. There are many practices I would not want to return to. But we have lost some of the good qualities of practice. *Morgan – Probation Manager*

Some probation officers felt that the closer relation with the prison service was a factor in increasing workloads:

When I came into public protection I walked into a caseload of 35 of high risk and at the moment it's about 48. Most of those are in prison but the prisons are putting more and more onto us and doing less even with lifers. So NOMS has led to us taking over some of the prison rehabilitation role. It doesn't make sense. *Sophie – Probation Officer*

Similarly, as Nash and Williams (2008) observe, the separation (in May 2007) of the Home Office and the Ministry of Justice has resulted in probation and police being moved into the spheres of responsibility of separate government departments. Liaison concerning core activities such as police intelligence gathering and supervising dangerous offenders by probation will be made much more difficult by this separation and will increase the amount of effort needed to make strong partnerships that work.

Somewhere in this mesh of relationships will be a potentially dangerous offender and up-to-date knowledge about him and of him will remain crucial to his effective supervision and management in the community (Nash & Williams 2008: 174).

As regards MAPPA, resource constraints and work overload pressurise practitioners to prioritise their own agencies, whatever the rules and procedures say. A probation officer described to me how he felt that he was completing all the preparations to present a case to MAPPA but other agencies were reluctant to help him with any resources.

> You go there *[MAPPA]* and you present the case, give a massive overview, doing most of the talking most of the time, everyone is there shaking their heads, agreeing with you, looks at the risk management plan, agrees it's sufficient and then basically signs it off and you're shown the exit. And you feel unsatisfied, you feel there should be more to MAPPA. From my point of view, I may go there with an offender I have been managing in an approved premises for six months and now it's time to move them on and I've come up with a dead-end in terms of housing. You know I go to a MAPPA meeting and there's a housing representative there and also the police that can check the address and you go there wanting some support in order to get that person moved on, practical support, and you come away with nothing. You come away with agencies continuing to be quite defensive...As practitioners you want support, where you have, say, an offender with say a personality disorder, you have got a specialist there, but they are not then having the time to be giving you support. You feel very much on your own as a practitioner. It's very unsatisfactory so I guess that's my experience. And I guess the team that I work with, they share similar experiences to me. *Simon – Probation Officer*

As far as Simon is concerned structures such as MAPPA add little apart from a greater complexity and burden on the probation officer.

> I think it's about committed individuals more than organizations. The process has become more complicated and the process is led by administrators anyway because the referral forms are a lot more extensive and there is a greater need now for a lot of the information you may put in a MAPPA referral, to relate to...police systems. The police will extract information from the MAPPA referrals and put it straight on their system. I think they feel they benefit: they get information but for you as a practitioner you spend a lot longer preparing for these meetings gathering information on paper and coming away with nothing. What tends to happen is because of the amount of cases being

discussed you've got to saturation point. So if you've got a guy, come out, you've referred him beforehand you've got him to the point of release, he's caught now in an approved premises, he's there and he's settled. The offender manager may still have a lot of anxiety about the case. But what the MAPPA will do, is think: he's out, stable, there's no ongoing issues so what we're going to do is drop him now to a 'level 1' so we don't need to hear about him anymore and it's all again still on your shoulders, and it's your responsibility. And you think well, has anything really been achieved through going through this process? Apart from having a few actions which you will have met anyway throughout the course of doing the work. *Simon – Probation Officer*

One of the aims of MAPPA was to standardise the way offenders are managed collaboratively between agencies around the country in terms of consistent assessments of risk but various factors work to undermine this. Particularly after Sonnex levels of referral of offenders to MAPPA have tended to increase as probation managers have erred on the side of caution and referred many offenders 'just in case', thereby reducing the resources available for the 'critical few' who do pose a real risk. Resource inequalities between areas mean that:

MAPPA doesn't really give you any standardisation in the sense you could have an armed robber who comes out (on licence) and in Kent is managed at a level 2, in London will more likely be managed at level 1. Because of the volume of cases. Is this really risk-management? Is this really public protection? *Simon – Probation Officer*

Furthermore the belief in the 'scientific' reliability of modern risk assessment procedures (of which more presently) tends to lower public tolerance of mistakes and errors (see Nash & Williams 2008). Public and media expectations then combine with high referral levels to make the work of MAPPA erratic and inconsistent not only between regions but between categories of offenders. Simon again:

What I've found is that sex offenders are managed a lot more rigidly than violent offenders. Why is that? They're probably less likely to commit another offence whilst subject to licence, they're more likely to comply and abide but why this disparity in terms of management? Maybe that's all about public anxieties and agencies almost feeling they have to manage certain offenders in certain ways. It doesn't leave you as a practitioner very confident when you've got a sex offender constantly being managed at level 2 that you're not really worried about because they're settled in a hostel, whilst you've got a violent offender who the MAPPA don't want to discuss anymore...You get the impression from the media that if somebody is appropriately managed in a multi-agency environment, that everything should be contained and everything should be working well. But you're kind of left with the feeling that this is not really true. It's still something that very much falls upon an individual's shoulders and if anything went wrong it will be the offender manager's fault. *Simon – Probation Officer*

The tenor of such remarks is that formalised procedures such as MAPPA cannot automatically produce either the necessary resources or the commitment of agencies and indeed, through greater bureaucratisation, may in fact erect obstacles to the multi-agency management of offenders. No amount of systems will replace committed individuals. The newer formalised collaboration procedures are still entirely dependent on committed individuals to make them work, just as the newer computerised risk assessment forms rely in fact on individuals who can take an experienced eye to the offender in order to fill them in properly. These systems fail precisely at the point at which individual commitment is overwhelmed by deskilling and under-resourcing, just as risk assessments fail at the point of under-resourced, deskilled practitioners being held responsible for completing them and acting on them. Indeed, the question of the *quality* of the information coming to these agencies and being 'shared or not' can easily be avoided when the focus is on the processes of co-ordination rather than what is being co-ordinated. This takes us straight to the heart of the debate about the measurement of risk. Before moving to the latter issue we need to look at how multi-agency collaboration has fared in the area of child protection. As a probation manager pointed out, the proliferation of multi-agency risk management does not guarantee effectiveness:

> What has changed from the 70s and 80s is the number of systems to support…risk management. The proliferation of different systems. MARACs, MAPPA, Safeguarding children, safeguarding adults, how do they relate to each other? If you have a violent person who has been arrested and charged with serious violence but you also know there is domestic abuse, there are child protection issues, how do you manage those complex cases? Theoretically if MAPPA is managing them, then MAPPA should coordinate it. As yet we are unclear how you move from one process to another. There are risks as well as benefits with these proliferated systems. And the danger is the potential for gaps or lack of communication between the different systems. *Morgan – Probation Manager*

Trust between agencies is all important in enabling multi-agency collaboration to work. For some probation practitioners the Sonnex case has undermined their credibility in the eyes of other agencies:

> I think trust in probation assessments has been lost by other agencies due to the Sonnex case. I had a sex offender who had been convicted of having obscene images on computer. He had a dream where he was having sex with someone who turned round and had his daughter's face. He was very disturbed by this and told me and I revised his risk assessment but still felt he did not pose too high risk to have access to his child. Nevertheless I reported the circumstances to Social Services. They reacted by putting restrictions on him and they requested an independent risk assessment be undertaken by a private psychologist firm to reassess the case implying my first assessment was not 'good enough'. The psychologist agreed with my assessment. But this proved to me that probation are no longer trusted by other agencies as much as before following the Sonnex case, and this can undermine the confidence felt by practitioners in their clinical judgements. Probation sells itself and its staff as experts in risk assessment, and if I'm honest that is what a good probation officer

is, yet this professionalism and clinical judgement is questioned and scrutinised continuously, by management and now partnership agencies. We have lost the confidence in our professional judgement. *Damien – Probation Officer*

A second factor undermining confidence in professional judgement is the increasing role of solicitors acting for offenders to challenge risk assessments by probation officers.

I had a case where a sex offender challenged, via one of these solicitors, their conditions and risk levels. When I refused to change my professional assessment, the solicitor demanded a new probation officer be allocated. The new officer was less experienced and also knew of this challenge to the previous assessment and therefore felt uncertain re: assessment and reduced the risk level as a consequence. The offender got what he wanted by using a solicitor to challenge my assessment and when I stood my ground I was replaced with a less experienced and less confident person. The Senior Probation Officer (SPO) in charge of the Public Protection team in which I work, received 33 letters from solicitors either challenging risk/conditions or demanding change of officer, in just one week in May 2010. I think this practice is worrying and very time consuming, diverting SPOs away from their busy duties to answer queries from solicitors intent on undermining their professional autonomy and judgement. How can poor behaviour be challenged when any confrontation the offender complains and gets what they want? *Damien – Probation Officer*

Child protection

Current arrangements for multi-agency work in child protection date from the Children's Act 1989 which provided the legislative framework for a *child protection register* intended as a record of all children in a local authority area for whom there were issues of neglect, physical injury, sexual or emotional abuse. All children placed on the register would have a *child protection plan* which was the basis for multi-agency collaboration and exchange of information. The fora for such exchange would involve periodic review conferences embracing police, local authority social services, health and education authorities depending on the nature of the neglect. All agencies work within a *common assessment framework*. Child protection issues can be taken to MAPPA in cases where, for example, a violent or sex offender is involved.

Social workers are generally in favour of multi-agency working:

> There is much more joined up multi-agency working. That has always been in child protection, if you called a child protection conference the multi agency network were called to that conference. But outside of child protection now there's more multi-agency working, and more early intervention work to try and prevent, to intervene with children in need at an earlier stage. I think generally multi agency working works better now. Clearly it doesn't always work, because if you think about Baby P. because information that needed to be shared throughout the network was not being shared as efficiently as it should be. As a general principle multi-agency working is the right way to go. *Beth – Social Worker*

> I think there is a desire now to work in a real integrated way, in the past there was idea of working with other agencies but agencies didn't know what each other did. I feel it is a strive towards more understanding. I think there is a drive, I am part of a drive as I work in a multi-agency team. It was a move to start working with education, social work, health in a team together. My manager is an education welfare officer and the team is social workers, education welfare officers, a parenting officer and a health team member once it is worked out by the services. We are a child in need team but we do pickup child protection cases. We are involved in family support panels, we have a worker in a children's centre, we go out to meet partnership agencies to enable all the agencies working with children to really work with each other. In the past we existed in our little pockets but didn't actually work together. *Kristy – Social Worker*

But as with the experience of some of the probation officers, there is often a feeling of other agencies simply 'dumping' issues on social work:

> It's like the Friday afternoon phone call where someone from another agency rings up saying I'm really worried about the

child, gives you details and then ends quickly by putting the phone down. I've handed it over to you the social worker now you manage it. Young social workers I talk to lie in bed at night anxiously worrying have I done the right thing. *Kristy – Social Worker*

And many felt this was part of a general devaluation of social work which had affected the outlook of other agencies:

As a profession there needs to be a shift in the way social workers are viewed. In all the care proceedings you ever go to experts are asked to do assessments of children and their parents and report to the court. And social workers aren't regarded as experts in the same way. If they have the primary relationship with a family, and they see that family day in, day out and week in, week out and they have meaningful relationships, why is their assessment not regarded in the same way to be an expert as say a psychiatrist? Respect and standing needs to improve. *Emma – Social Worker Manager*

The whole kind of perception of social workers needs to change. Social workers need to be seen as the experts, which at one time I think, they were regarded as. I think we've been de-skilled. *Beth – Social Worker*

There was an understanding, as in probation, that effective multiagency work depends on good relations between individuals in the different agencies. At the same time some of the social workers interviewed detected blind spots in probation attitudes to child protection:

We often find that probation professionals do not consider the children even if they're living with a violent offender. They don't even bother to ask if they have children and suddenly they say 'oh they've got children, do we need to work together to consider the risk?' *Pippa – Social Worker Manager*

If you have particular links with individuals, say in a mental health team that are positive, you can call on them for guidance and information about where you can get expert advice or call upon their duty worker, for the information. I think if strong links aren't there it gets difficult. I do think, and you mention probation it's difficult sometimes to get probation officers to child protection conferences and the core groups that have to happen because I think their specialism is in probation and they see their main kind of focus as the adult whereas in fact they are part of the network that needs to work together to ensure a child is being safeguarded. I think it's always going to be a challenge having good multiagency working and I can think of many examples where it works very well and others where for different reasons key people in those networks, don't work as effectively with our children social workers. *Emma – Social Worker Manager*

However something which social work may have in common with probation is the extent to which recent organisational developments may well have undermined as much as reinforced multi-agency collaboration. In his report into the death of Victoria Climbié, Lord Laming made two crucial recommendations, the first being that the child protection register be phased out and that the government 'actively explore' the possibility of a more generalised preventative approach governing all children. Laming came to this conclusion after studying the failure of agencies to collaborate effectively in the Climbié case. Yet the problem may not have been the child protection register. In the opinion of Liz Davies and Nora Duckett the register:

> provided a confidential alert system to hospitals and police facilitating the identification of particularly vulnerable children and enabling swift intervention to protect them. Studies of serious case reviews demonstrated that few children who died had been on the Child Protection Register (Davies & Duckett 2008: 165; see also Gillen 2008).

The problems facing the new prevention oriented children database and the Children's Act 2004 have been discussed in the previous chapter but the specific issue of the subsuming of child protection into this all-embracing preventative approach (the database has been abolished by the Coalition Government largely on the grounds of its intrusiveness) may well have made it more rather than less difficult to identify vulnerable children and take action. This was certainly Davies' opinion:

> With a 30-year career in child protection, I know the register has been invaluable in flagging up those at grave risk....The database replacing it aims to log intimate details about all children. Social workers say vulnerable children are now lost like needles in a haystack (Davies 2009).

In any case, by the time of Baby Peter not much seemed to have changed. The new preventative approach had not produced closer liaison between agencies and the case was marked by a lack of co-ordination between social work, medical services and the police. As Laming's report of 2009 observed:

> ...it is evident that the challenges of working across organ- isational boundaries continue to pose barriers in practice, and that cooperative efforts are often the first to suffer when services and individuals are under pressure (Laming 2009: 37).

The doctor didn't recognise the symptoms of injury and didn't report them to social services when the foster carer took Baby Peter to the surgery. No amount of formalisation of multi-agency working or preventative databases is going to prevent such mistakes occur- ring when the real issue is the quality of information being gathered in the first place.

Meanwhile a second key recommendation of Laming's 2003 report on Victoria Climbié also created, it has been argued, addi- tional obstacles to efficient multi-agency collaboration. It was noted in the previous chapter that Laming had recommended that the police concentrate on criminal investigations. This may well have resulted, as argued in the previous chapter, in additional resource distribution within the police and away from child protection work. Under the 1989 Children Act, social workers and police collaborated to investigate suspicions of 'actual or likely significant harm' to a child but Laming's 2003 recommendation that police should only investigate crime and not the risk of significant harm means that social workers are less likely to work closely with police. The result was that in the Baby Peter case:

> Unexplained injuries, suspicious marks, medical findings, forensic evidence, sibling interviews, parental accounts and investigation of other known adults, were not jointly analysed by police and social workers working together. Police information about previous crimes by adults in the household was not shared and remained unknown to the social workers. Although Peter Connolly's name was on the child protection register, the child protection conferences were poorly informed by assessments rather than investigations. In court the social worker for Peter Connolly defined her role as to support the family rather than to protect the child (Davies 2010: 32).

Increasing the separation of police and social work parallels the separation that some probation officers identified as resulting from the division between the Home Office and the Ministry of Justice. The most important issue of all however was identified by one of the social workers interviewed:

> You cannot deal with a child in isolation, you have to look at them in relation to the other kind of aspects in their personality, their needs, the environment in which they are living, and who the caregivers are and their needs. You need a much more holistic view of the child and their context. *Beth – Social Worker*

The notion of a holistic view is key. The most fundamental aspect of 'what practitioners really do' involves the quality of information actually being collected and the question of how far can it be used as a reliable basis for constructing a view of a child in danger, or of a serious offender, which may enable the practitioner to make a realistic assessment.

The risk agenda

An element of the task of practitioners in both probation and social work was always the assessment of the risk of something dangerous happening. However, the proliferation of social fragmentation and intensification of public insecurity about crime and violence (Young 1999; Garland 2001; Lea 2002) have acted to shift the focus of agencies such as prisons, probation and social work away from the *rehabilitation of* offenders and people in various categories of trouble towards the prioritisation of the *protection of the public from* such people. This focus on public protection has led to the prioritisation of the assessment of risk – of offenders committing further crimes, or of children being abused.

Traditional psycho-analytically derived casework methods in both social work and probation (and at one time of course probation officers *were* social workers) have become increasingly displaced by formalised 'tick-box' computerised risk assessment systems which allocate a 'risk score' epitomised by the OASys in probation or the ICS in child protection social work. The deployment of these systems has a profound effect on 'what practitioners actually do'. They change the relationship between the practitioner and the client or offender; they change the type of information gathered by the former about the latter; they change the image of the client or offender held by the practitioner and, most important of all, they profoundly change the skills and methods of work of the practitioner. The understanding of the effect of these methods may well yield up the answer to the question of why practitioners seem to make the same 'mistakes' irrespective of injunctions to practitioners to 'do what you are supposed to' issued by Lord Laming and numerous other bureaucrats.

In traditional casework methods formerly deployed by both social work and probation, much accountability lay in the relationship of trust established between practitioner and client crucial to the strategies of therapy, guidance and rehabilitation (Vanstone 2004a). Codes of ethics related to social work practice and probation casework typically placed accountability to clients centre stage and before responsibilities to employing agencies (Burton and Van Den Broek 2009: 1326). This key relationship, both in probation and social work, has been displaced by a concern with the management of the risk presented by the client (Froggett 2002; Goodman 2003; Hudson 2001, 2003; Kemshall 2003; Nellis 2004; Oldfield 2002; Robinson 2003a, 2003b, 2005). Accountability has shifted from the relationship between the practitioner and the client, essential from the standpoint of rehabilitation, to the public and to the audit of efficiency (Munro 2004) essential from the standpoint of public protection in relation to which the client or offender becomes increasingly marginalised.

In both the Sonnex and Baby Peter cases risk assessments played a key role. In the Sonnex case a consequence of the failure of multiagency communication between prison and probation was that he ended up with inaccurate risk scores. Mistakes were certainly made. However, a further issue is how far Sonnex's behaviour could have been predicted even from a consistent and rigorous OASys assessment. In a similar way it can be argued that social workers in the Baby Peter case failed to assess correctly the risks to his life, despite the amount of time they spend at their computers entering data on risk. Again, the social workers involved made mistakes, but behind this lies the issue of whether even the most attentive tick-box risk assessments can actually be a valid guide to what is likely to happen. There are fundamental issues about risk assessment in both social work and probation that cannot simply be put down to individual failure and poor communications: in particular whether risk assessments as currently conceived contain key blind spots that weaken them as methods for anticipating the behaviour of people like Sonnex or from ringing alarm bells in situations like that of Baby Peter. Practitioners are continually less likely to know what is going on, not because they are lazy or fail to follow procedures, but because those very procedures involve reorganisation and retraining in ways which make it harder to know what is really happening.

The first obvious way in which practitioners lose contact with what is going on is simply that they spend an increasing amount of their time in front of the computer screen updating risk assessment schedules. The choice between working longer (unpaid) hours or losing contact with the client through lack of time is a real one.

> Some social workers go far beyond what's expected of them but I think they spend maybe 65 or 60 percent of their time in front of the computer. It feels like an enormous amount of time is spent with people sitting at computers looking at the Integrated Children's System and completing that. As a senior practitioner I spend a large amount of time sitting in front of the computer

these days. Maybe 50 percent of my time as a senior practitioner is in front of the computer. It does feel like more time is spent sat in front of the computers these days, than doing face-to-face work. If practitioners want to do meaningful face to face work they end up increasingly spending longer hours trying to keep on top of case notes etc., doing extra unpaid hours is a way that social workers manage to keep on top of their work. It's very rare that in my team people ever leave on time, people work longer hours. Because of the hype and publicity in more recent times about social workers I think maybe people spend longer hours because they are more anxious about covering their backs most of the time. But also being able to evidence the positive work they're trying to do. The positive work they do with families is evidenced on their records. *Emma – Social Work Manager*

In child protection the replacement of the Child Protection Register by the mammoth tick-box surveillance system of the ICS aiming at the registration of all children (now discontinued by the Coalition Government) could not have been better designed to distract practitioners from a focus on children at risk:

Professionals overwhelmed with meeting performance targets, responding to low level concerns, preoccupied with data entry, and under pressure to close cases within predefined timescales for assessments, find it difficult to focus their attention on children at risk of harm (Davies & Duckett 2008: ix).

Davies and Duckett also refer to research by the University of York on social workers' reactions to the ICS. One report on this research revealed the reactions of social workers in the following terms:

As they saw it, the standard headings lack the flexibility required to reflect the needs of differing groups of children, promoting instead a classified, repetitive and disconnected description and not a coherent, specific analysis of what should be done. Its time limits aim at a business-like approach. But is accurate information on (say) identity available within five days of first contact? In these ways, the social workers felt that the system had failed to take account of their particular needs, saw it as far too prescriptive, and, for the most part, were not committed to it (Shaw et al. 2009: 623).

The researchers continued that social workers did not feel that the ICS undermined their autonomy, but 'they varied in what they recorded, how they understood cases and how they practised' (Shaw et al. 2009: 623). This means simply that the system is not enforced and that many social workers retain their ability to use traditional skills. Indeed social workers retaining the older casework skills are probably the only ones capable of showing this autonomy just as probation officers with these skills are the people capable of making OASys assessments remotely approaching reality.

In both social work and probation the survival of the older case-work skills among the majority of practitioners is endangered by new training methods and deskilling. New occupational grades of relatively deskilled Social Work Assistants and Probation Service Officers have been introduced in recent years.

> In my team we have three social workers and two social work assistants. I see a trend of social work assistants taking on really quite complex work. Given that they're not qualified. They have no training at all. I think it needs to be talked about. If social work assistants are very good, they're learning as they go along. But they were meant to come in and do a job supporting social workers and then go on to do the training themselves. What's happening is that social work assistants are coming in at low pay and then they get to take on really complex work. One day it will kind of bite somebody in the arse. I think this needs to be raised now because if it is not raised that will be a disaster. I have to give work to people who have not had the training, why should they be doing such complex work? They should be supporting social workers not what they do, they carry their own case load of complex work...It's a disservice to those who have done the training because just saying the job can be done by someone without the training. I feel that social workers have to collec-tively challenge this practice. In the job description for a social work assistant it says they should not take on complex cases but none of the cases we deal with are not complex!! Interestingly, the job description does not define 'non complex'. I feel this is

done because once you define 'complex' you won't be able to use your staff base. *Pippa – Social Work Manager*

Meanwhile in probation a new division of labour has emerged in which skilled and experienced officers concentrate on very high risk cases (and thus tend to have high caseloads almost exclusively of demanding high risk offenders) while low or medium risk offenders (80 percent of all offenders) are supervised by the newer grade of semi-skilled Probation Service Officers (PSOs) (Fitzgibbon 2009). Sonnex presented as in many ways a model client – his attendance at supervision meetings was punctual; he was well turned out and co-operative. He ticked all the boxes. Problems might have been identified earlier if he had been closely scrutinised by a more experienced practitioner. This is because the experienced practitioner, whether in social work or probation, will have developed knowledge and experience (and possibly experienced some of the older casework training) which will enable them to take a holistic view of the client in their environment and develop knowledge which goes beyond the simple categorised information of 'tick-box' risk assessment. This is important precisely because it is well known, at least to probation practitioners, that risk assessment scores are not a reliable guide to the likely behaviour of offenders. This is for three reasons.

First, research by Ansbro (2006) and Craissati and Sindall (2009) shows that that low or medium risk offenders can go on to commit serious further offences and that risk is a dynamic evolving phenomenon. Craissati and Sindall, from a study of a sample of SFOs, concluded that:

SFOs...tend to be committed by a heterogeneous group including a number of low to medium risk offenders, many of whom are on community sentences and most of whom are not considered high enough risk to be discussed by the MAPPP (2009: 24).

They concluded that the most important factor in precipitation of an SFO was not the characteristics of the offenders themselves as would be predicted by risk assessments, however sophisticated these may be, but rather the 'situational contexts' within which the offenders found themselves. These were most likely to precipitate further offences such as 'angry disputes, usually between men, in situations where pride and status are exposed and challenged and vengeance is sought' (2009: 25).

In other words what the probation officer or social worker needs to know is less his or her client's risk score than the type of social situations into which they are likely to get themselves or, in Parton's (2008) terms, less 'informational' and more 'social' knowledge. This, of course, points back to the old skilled casework, once common to probation and social work, in which it was the first job of the practitioner to *know their client* and to acquire knowledge about the social world in which the client moved by *walking the walk*. It points in exactly the opposite direction to the world of the over-worked, under-resourced, partially de-skilled practitioner whose only knowledge of the client, among the hundred or so on the caseload, is the risk score.

A similar point has been made about the new computerised risk assessment systems in child protection: that there is little scope for recording the 'situational contexts' which are the real key to an understanding of whether a child is in danger. A study of the methodology of the Common Assessment Framework, used alongside the ICS in children's services, observes:

> What becomes apparent is that the structure of the Core Assessment encourages a fragmented view of 'the family'. The child is constructed through a series of boxes which list 'needs'. Parents or carers are constructed in terms of how they address those needs, and parental attributes are seen in terms of deficits and difficulties. There is nowhere to write about relations with siblings or friends, except in negative terms under 'family functioning', where 'The young person's impairment/behaviour has a negative impact on siblings'. The child is viewed as having a set of attributes and problems, but these are to be reported in isolation from issues concerning their families or communities (Hall et al. 2010: 403).

Is it any wonder that social workers make mistakes when saddled with systems that take them away from a holistic understanding of clients in their environments?

Secondly, the problem with tick-box risk assessment appears all the more obvious when the statistical nature of such methods is further considered. Robinson (2003a) makes the point that actuarial methods of risk assessment deployed in probation are 'both based on and designed for use with groups or *populations* of offenders. This means that they cannot provide accurate predictions of risk in respect of individuals' (Robinson 2003a: 116). The score registered for an individual client indicates simply that the client belongs to a group which has a *statistical probability* of certain types of behaviour. Whether that individual actually will engage in such behaviour is still a question for the individual judgement of the practitioner (Horsfield 2003) and, therefore, the better the practitioner knows the individual client the more accurate that judgement is likely to be. Where the practitioner does not have an intimate knowledge of the client then the characteristics of the group will be translated into the characteristics of the individual following 'the tendency to view everyone as a potential threat, in which the worst is suspected until proven otherwise' (McLaughlin 2006: 10). The *ecological fallacy*, well known to statisticians, observes that the characteristics of individuals cannot be inferred from the characteristics of areas or groups. In risk analysis there is thus the very real possibility of an *actuarial fallacy* whereby the behaviour of individuals is spuriously inferred from the behaviour of groups. Brian Littlechild (2008) reinforces this point by comparing the use of risk analysis in motor insurance and social work:

> Thus, in relation to driving a car, for example, risks to different age groups, dependent upon where they live, previous offences and accidents, etc., are collected and analysed over time. However, actuarial approaches do not try to predict or manage risk to individual drivers; they balance the risk to their business having to settle claims from drivers by assessing the likelihood of the number of individuals from within certain groups making claims on their insurance. What they do not try to do is to predict which individual, over a period of time, will make that claim on their insurance. In health and social care professions, this is what it appears that agencies and professionals are expected to do (Littlechild 2008: 668).

The result is a tendency towards inflation taking the form of over-prediction of dangerousness of individuals, such dangerousness being conflated with the risk characteristics for the group to which the individual has been allocated (see Kemshall 2003; Warner & Gabe 2006; Fitzgibbon 2008).

Finally, the combination of downgrading of older casework skills and increasing practitioner workloads impedes the ability to complete even the risk assessments with any degree of reliability (Milner & O'Byrne 1998). Where there is institutionalised pressure to complete assessments under conditions of resource constraints and lack of training in traditional casework skills all manner of subjective judgements creep into assessments (Webb 2006). For example, assessors frequently question their ability to expand clinically on the assessment and resort to 'just getting the job done' (Maynard-Moody et al. 1990). Even practitioners who want to undertake in-depth assessments are prohibited by the process and time restrictions imposed by targets.

> I am forced to submit my OASys assessment within the time scale provided and once submitted the assessment is 'locked'. So if when I meet the offender again and get to know him more and realize some other facts about his situation I am not able to add this information into the OASys. All because the time-line does not fit with my getting to know my offender. *Steve – Probation Officer*

These issues are also present in child protection. Broadhurst et al. (2010) make the point that the ability of practitioners to go beyond the formalised risk assessments is:

> undermined by a central government tendency to over-prescribe, leaving less scope for local developments that are worker and service user-led. Reinforced through an inspection regime that focuses on compliance with national targets and procedures, practitioners can be left floundering with poorly designed tools. So, if time-scales promote speed and electronic workflows prioritise completion, as is the case of current 'ICS-enabled' practices of child welfare in England and Wales, then judgements are being made on slender grounds (Broadhurst et al. 2010: 1049; see also Munro 2004).

Harry Ferguson echoes the same point:

> Levels of performance management and bureaucratization of social work are, if anything, intensifying in the 2000s, as more horrific

cases of abuse and organizational failure are publicly disclosed, the workers involved are blamed, named and shamed, yet more performance management targets are imposed by government and new information technologies provide more scope for standardization and organizational control of workers (Ferguson 2010: 1104).

Ferguson calls for a renewed focus not solely on *systems risk* but on *practice risks* and the individual social worker's unique experience of doing social work with another unique individual in their home or social context. He recognises how caseload and organisation priorities mitigate against this. Quoted in a newspaper article referring to the Baby Peter case he noted:

the striking thing about what is known about his case is how skilfully deceitful the mother and male cohabitants were in concealing the child's injuries. This is known in the child protection literature as 'disguised compliance', where superficial co-operation is a front for concealing abuse....The energy devoted to organisational reforms such as children's trusts and the emphasis on service users rights in social work education must no longer be allowed to divert attention from providing social workers with the knowledge and supports that are essential to performing such personally and professionally demanding work (Benjamin 2008).

There is a need to continually think 'outside the risk-score':

Taking things to the...multiagency risk assessment conferences for domestic violence that we have. You're scoring people but one of the things they've always said, is do the score but don't just think about the score. If you think something warrants our attention but it doesn't add up in the score when you're doing the tick-box exercise, its still fine to bring it, that's important. I'm not saying you shouldn't use risk assessment tools but you have to have the common sense to know when to think outside those rules. They're a guide not this is all you have to do. Like these assessments we had to do they were prescribed but there was a tick-box section and we got rid of it. All it does is reduce things to yes or no and what does that tell you? It's important that people write down what they're thinking. *Kristy – Social Worker*

This amounts to the admission that it is only possible to work by using methods which are not part of the procedures. Yet, as we have seen, when disasters like Baby Peter or Sonnex occur, the first response of the management is to tighten the procedures. A different approach might be to spend more time studying why it is that practitioners need to go beyond the procedures and to see what it is that is lacking in the procedures themselves. It is not possible in the long term to rely on the skills of practitioners to go 'beyond the risk-score'. Sooner or later it is necessary to confront the issue of what are the best working methods. If this is not done then gradually the shift, identified by Parton (2008) as from 'social' to 'informational' and by Aas (2004) as from 'narrative' to 'database' becomes permanent. The client becomes deconstructed into a bundle of risks and the holistic picture is lost.

In probation the ascendancy of public protection over rehabilitation legitimises the deconstruction of the client into a bundle of risks. A holistic knowledge of the offender based on narrative; biography and situational context are highly relevant from the standpoint of the reintegration of the individual into society. Although, as previously noted, risk scores are not in actual fact reliable predictors of re-offending, the status of the offender as 'threatening other' facilitates the backgrounding of biography and context in favour of a set of *characteristics of the offender* described as 'criminogenic needs' and classified, in the OASys system, by reference to a complex of factors including previous and current offence(s) and the potential for harm to self or members of the public which such offences indicate. A number of background factors are included such as accommodation, education, employment, financial situation, relationships, lifestyle and associates, drug and alcohol misuse, emotional well-being, thinking and behaviour, attitudes, health and other considerations. OASys then allocates a score between 0 and 2 (2 being a serious problem) and then guides the practitioner to the level and type of intervention required by the offender profile (Home Office 2002). What is not recognised is that this factorising approach to aspects of the offender's situation constitutes not a contextualisation but rather in itself a decontextualisation of the offender and imposes limits on the knowledge available about him or her.

Having been deconstructed into a bundle of risk scores, the offender is then reconstructed as a complex of criminogenic needs which then require cognitive skills training to enable those needs to be managed. The emphasis is primarily on training offenders to adjust to their circumstances and keep quiet (i.e. cease to engage in criminality or risky behaviour). As Hannah-Moffat puts it:

> This construction of the offender leaves intact the presumption that crime is the outcome of poor choices or decisions, and not the outcome of structural inequalities or pathology. The offender's poor decisions were a consequence of an absence or of deficiencies in requisite skills, abilities, and attitudes necessary for proper informed decision-making (2005: 42).

Offending is here portrayed in terms of *failure* to make rational choice rather than as the *outcome* of rational choice, let alone as a revolt against that very rationality of the social system which appears to have put the offender in his initial predicament (Young 2003). Thus in the currently deployed OASys template criminogenic need scores will be enhanced if the client exhibits 'a great deal of antipathy towards the legal system and agencies', 'justifies own behaviour by comparisons with misdemeanours of others', 'favours or excuses criminal behaviour regularly and with conviction', or 'expresses views supportive of offending at any time in interview' (Home Office 2002: 109).

Since social work is not concerned with criminal offenders *per se* but with a wider spectrum of individuals and families facing a variety of problems, the scope for the expansion of tick-box technology and the deconstruction of all sorts of individuals living tragic and difficult lives into a variety of risk characteristics is immensely greater. In children's services, from *Every Child Matters* until the closure of the ContactPoint database – which aimed at the registration of *every* child – the practitioner was faced with a vast computerised system comprising the ContactPoint database through which practitioners could see which other practitioners were working with the same child, the Common Assessment Framework which would record young people with additional needs and the Integrated

Children's System which contained data on children at risk under the terms of the Children's Act 1989. Child protection social workers were thus heavily involved with the latter database and as already noted above that the data entry system obstructs a holistic view of situational contexts. This, as Munro suggested, might have been the reason why Haringey was given a clean bill of health in the first Ofsted report, prior to the one specially commissioned by Ed Balls, despite the death of Baby Peter. The ICS has produced:

> a system that is bureaucratically perfect – literally, no one is to blame – and humanly a nightmare....As the LSE's Eileen Munro noted: 'Haringey had a beautiful paper trail of how they failed to protect this baby...The ICS fails on all counts. So, yes, heads should probably roll over the awful death of Baby P. It's just that they are not the ones most people think should roll' (Caulkin 2008).

In such conditions when things go wrong the focus is precisely on the risk assessment programme. If the client has been deconstructed into a database of risk scores (Aas 2004; Parton 2008) then the only issue is 'were the boxes filled in correctly?' rather than, for example, why wasn't Sonnex seen by any experienced practitioners?; why didn't Baby Peter's social workers develop a more sophisticated knowledge of the family and its environment?

The focus on 'were the risk-scores correctly completed or not?' automatically shifts power to management at the expense of practitioners. This has two effects. Firstly it encourages a defensiveness on the part of front line practitioners. Relations start to become 'workers versus bosses' rather than a 'flat hierarchy' of skilled professionals. This has already been noted in Parton's characterisation of the defensiveness of social workers at the Climbié inquiry. More recently, following the Baby Peter case, Munro makes the point that management gets the blame from the media (and, as we have seen, from politicians) and transmits this down the chain to the front line practitioners:

> The defensive, controlling style of management is an understandable reaction to the level of blame from society when children die. However, it is a response that inadvertently encourages

people to place the protection of themselves and their agencies above the protection of children (Munro 2010a: 1149).

No amount of informal 'working beyond the risk-score' can defend against this when a crisis occurs. The end result is not simply the establishment of 'shop floor' relations in social services and probation offices but the deskilling of the practitioner as the mirror image of the deconstruction of the client. Once the client has disappeared into the maze of tick-boxes, then the old casework skills of social workers and probation officers to develop an in-depth knowledge of the client become redundant. The practitioner becomes a box-ticker, more at home in front of the computer screen than walking the walk. This deskilling takes the initial form of work reorganisation, a new division of labour and the employment of new categories of semi-skilled operatives.

There is evidence from primary research studies conducted by the author (Fitzgibbon & Green 2006; Fitzgibbon 2007, 2008; Fitzgibbon et al. 2010) suggesting that the current over-reliance on OASys risk assessment techniques is part of the attempt to replace skilled practitioners with semi-skilled operatives. Similar developments are under way in social work (White et al. 2009; Hall et al. 2010) but eventually all operatives become deskilled in the fact of new reorganisations of work and responsibilities. The deskilling of the probation officer is no more clearly illustrated than by the fact that prison officers can equally implement the risk analysis templates such as OASys. Such deskilling makes way for a fragmentation and differentiation of tasks and skills among probation officers. Robinson in her study of offender management found that:

> for example, staff *either* conducted assessments and wrote reports *or* delivered programmes, *or* managed 'public protection' (that is, high risk of harm) cases. This new style of delivering supervision was...based on a new understanding of offenders as 'actuarial subjects'....to be assessed and then 'managed into' appropriate resources (Robinson 2005: 309–310).

In interviews with newly qualified probation officers in 2008 the author found them to be more concerned with managerial processes, targets and tasks than with the offender or with their own relationship with the offender (Fitzgibbon 2008). There appeared to be more concern about whether the risk assessment was accurate than how the offender was managed and what was being done to reduce risk. Wildly inaccurate estimates of risk can result. Thus in one case:

> Whilst certain issues were acknowledged, the practitioner then skipped over the details and even failed to incorporate the history of depression into the OASys. These omissions were such that the local Psychiatric services contacted the probation officer on the mentally disordered offender's request. The practitioner had not noted deterioration in the offender's mental health despite seeing him regularly. Nor had they assisted in providing access to the appropriate help and services required by the offender. Even after these events these developments were not included in an OASys review and in fact these reviews were largely missing from file. This led to lack of appropriate support and finally the practitioner defensively inflated the risk estimation. This culminated in a short period in custody for breach of the attendance requirements of rehabilitation order with all the implications for loss of family ties, employment and housing (Fitzgibbon 2008: 94–95).

The paradox, as already highlighted, is that only a willingness to work outside the tick-box methods and grasp the 'situational context' in which clients and offenders are located, enables reliable estimates of real risk – practice risk as opposed to system risk in Ferguson's terminology to be made.

But working outside the tick-box culture is simply guerrilla resistance which will find it difficult to survive if the formal training procedures and organisational structures are all pointing in a different direction. However, it is clear that training regimes in probation have not entirely displaced a concern with the importance of relations of trust between practitioner and client. Even practitioners trained recently, where courses such as the Diploma in Probation Studies have moved towards centralising methods of working and utilising technology to monitor attendance, have not completely dismissed notions of relationship. Much recent research (Annison et al. 2008; McNeill 2006; Robinson & Burnett 2007), has shown that practice is still concerned with helping clients to change positively.

> It could be assumed that all that is required to resolve the disjuncture between the values of practitioners and their practice environment is to allow natural wastage to take its course and assume that as newly qualified practitioners join the service, they will automatically adopt technicist values that are more in keeping with the punitive managerialist mode of practice. However, evidence to date does not suggest this will be a straightforward process. This author's experience is that more recently qualified practitioners have been formally taught about the process of reflective practice during their training (Gregory 2010: 2288).

This has been reinforced by much of the academic research and discussion on the dynamics of desistance which has:

> highlighted that interventions (regardless of how well delivered) are still unlikely to 'work' unless the individual has reached a point whereby they themselves are able to move towards adopting a non offending or pro-social identity, in an environment that is supportive towards these goals, matched by the existence of wider structural opportunities (Burke 2010: 364).

There are at least three bodies of research that are the basis of a robust defence of the centrality of the relationship between practitioner and client in probation. First, the studies on the actual dynamics of desistance such as that by Maruna et al. (2004) who in their Liverpool Desistance Study concluded that the key to success or failure was less to do with appropriate programme referral based on the assessment of the client as a risk than with stressing the client's strengths and future potential such that:

> especially in efforts to reintegrate ex-prisoners back into society, it may make sense to balance such talk of risks and needs with an emphasis on the person's potential 'strengths' (Maruna et al. 2004: 228).

Offenders have to come to terms with their past. The best way to do this may be to get them to evaluate their own biographies and to use therapeutic techniques which focus on the 'whole individual' not just an artificial 'data-vidual' (Aas 2004) assembled from ticked boxes.

Such themes relate closely to the literature on 'pro-social modelling'. Developed by Australian psychologist Chris Trotter during the early 1990s (see Trotter 1999, 2004, 2009) pro-social modelling has been a technique known to probation for many years and was influential when enhanced community punishment was introduced in 2003–4 (HM Inspectorate of Probation 2006d). Much of Trotter's conception of the strategy appears familiar. He asks what probation officers should do to reinforce 'pro-social' (i.e. non-criminal) attitudes on the part of clients:

> The first and most obvious method of providing reinforcement is through body language (e.g. smiling, attentive listening, leaning forward) and the use of praise. Rewards can also be provided by the worker giving time to the client, attending court with the client and providing positive evidence, reducing the frequency of contact, helping the client find a job or accommodation, doing home visits or meeting a client outside the office, doing a positive report for a court or parole board, speaking to other agencies/professionals such as social security or the police about the client's needs and making positive comments in file notes (Trotter 2009: 141).

Helping the client find a job or accommodation relates directly to the research by Farrall and others, mentioned in Chapter 4 on the importance of community resources rather than cognitive skills as the key driver in desistance from crime. However important the interpersonal interaction, if the practitioner can get the offender into a worthwhile job then the chances of desistance are substantially increased. Of course both are important. The mere offer of employment may be insufficient if there is not already a supportive relationship:

> Desistance-supporting interventions need to...be based on legitimate and respectful relationships...to focus on social capital (opportunities) and...to exploit strengths as well as addressing needs and risks (McNeill 2006: 55).

Several other researchers have pointed to the dependence of rehabilitation and desistance, these qualities being retained within the client/practitioner relationship (see for example, Burnett 2004; Robinson 2005; Fitzgibbon 2007, 2008; Burnett & Maruna 2006; Maruna & Immarigeon 2004; Ansbro 2008; Barry 2007).

Maurice Vanstone entitles the last chapter of his book on the history of probation theory and practice (Vanstone 2004a) 'Back to Where We Started'. In stressing that successful probation work involves 'the ability to engage with the individual in a relationship founded on concreteness, empathy and commitment' (Vanstone 2004a: 157) he points to the recovery of the older social work tradition of probation expressed in the mantra 'advise, assist and befriend'. We have indeed come back to where we started, but unfortunately under totally different social, economic and political conditions.

There are, on the face of it, encouraging noises from the new government. In October 2010, in response to a parliamentary question, Crispin Blunt, Parliamentary Under-Secretary of State for Prisons and Probation, revealed:

> In December 2008, NOMS undertook a snapshot survey over a one-week period, based on a small sample of probation officer and probation service officer staff. It reported that across England and Wales 24 percent of PO/PSO time was spent in direct contact with offenders, 41 percent was involved in computer activity and 35 percent of time was spent on non-computer-dealing with correspondence, meetings, travel, etc. (Hansard 2010).

He announced that in response to this survey NOMS was:

> initiating the Offender Engagement Programme to evaluate and improve the quality of face to face work with offenders and its impact on reoffending, and identify and reduce any barriers to that work taking place (Hansard 2010).

Before evaluating the likelihood of such a development it is important to note briefly that very similar themes have emerged in child protection with a stress on the need to move the relationship between practitioner and client beyond the 'tick-box culture'. In an important recent contribution Eileen Munro (2010a) eloquently answers the question with which this chapter began: why do practitioners break the rules and fail to comply with procedures.

> Practitioners can break rules for good reason. The range of decision scenarios they confront is so varied that, at times, the rules or accepted good practice do not apply. Also, when there are constraints of time and resources in the system, workers have to make pragmatic decisions about what to prioritise...Therefore, the work environment can make it difficult or undesirable to follow the official procedure (Munro 2010a: 1138).

The main problem with the existing regime is that:

> compliance with existing procedures, rules and audit regimes is the key focus of appraisal rather than whether those procedures, rules and so on are the best way of protecting children (Munro 2010a: 1139).

So when things go wrong, as in the cases of Victoria Climbié, Baby Peter and others, the tendency, as exemplified by the Laming reports, is to respond by tightening up the rules and procedures. We have noted that this was also the response by probation to the Dano Sonnex case.

Munro is advocating the replacement of top-down management of cases through risk assessments by tick-box appraisals conducted by increasingly deskilled practitioners who have little time to get to know the reality of their client's lives. In its place she advocates a return to the centrality of the practitioner-client relationship in which the practitioner is free – and has time – to learn through reflective practice. The role of management in such a 'systems approach' is to learn from and adapt to practitioner learning and reflection in a negation of the assumption that management, through control of the procedures is the ultimate repository of wisdom. We need, Munro argues, to create a situation in which organisations such as social work can develop:

> good feedback loops so that senior management can learn of problems and facilitate adaptations to avoid them (Munro 2010a: 1149).

The implementation of such reforms raises crucial questions of organisational form and culture. To shift the accountability of the practitioner more in the direction of the client and away from management and audit requires a re-orientation of management to become itself part of a learning and feedback loop and to concentrate more on ensuring that front line practitioners are equipped with the skills and resources they need for their work with children and families. How would this be achieved?

Shortly after the death of Victoria Climbié a pamphlet from the *Demos* think-tank (Cooper et al. 2003) suggested re-organisation along the lines of decentralisation of social workers to multi-disciplinary teams based in schools, health centres and the community, where they could be governed by a 'non-managerial' form of supervision rather than the audit and computerised tick-box culture. They called for:

> more autonomy for individual social workers within a team so that they are given responsibility for their own work in a similar way to GPs (Cooper et al. 2003: 16).

This, they hoped, could lay the ground for a more relationship-based practice in which the professional authority and autonomy of the practitioner oriented to negotiation with the client and the establishment of trust rather than the recourse of the increasingly deskilled operative to compliance with prescribed procedures which may well miss what is happening under the noses of practitioners.

There have been innovations in one or two individual social services departments around the UK which have carried at least some of these ideas into effect. Cooper et al. refer to a project initiated by Nottingham City Social Services Department in 2000 which gave increased autonomy to social workers in service delivery. More recently, following the murder of two children by their mother, widely criticised as preventable if social workers had been doing their job, the London Borough of Hackney re-organised its children's services away from the hierarchical model:

> Instead of the usual hierarchy, with front-line social workers at the bottom, Hackney created a system of small units, each headed by a consultant social worker. These consultants are key. They are highly experienced, able, well-trained...The units include therapists, clinical practitioners, and co-ordinators. All work closely together on cases, with the consultant taking

responsibility, usually handling between 30 and 40 cases in all (Berg 2010).

It is undoubtedly easier for such innovations to take place in social services than probation. Social work is, by comparison, already decentralised in that it is organised at the Local Authority level while probation is part of the centralised NOMS. As noted above, some pilot projects are occurring as part of the Offender Engagement Programme but these will, most likely, have to be evaluated by the core bureaucracy before widespread adoption. There have indeed been some recent moves towards organisational decentralisation. The 2009 Offender Management Act enables high performing Probation Areas to become Trusts which deliver services under contract to NOMS with the Trust deciding the best way to deliver those services.

However this has to be seen in the context of contestability and the establishment of strategic partnerships with local voluntary and private sector providers as well as other criminal justice agencies. Privatisation raises a number of problems both for social work and probation which I shall consider in the next chapter. In particular, competition among private sector providers to secure contracts on the basis of 'payment by results' in an atmosphere of financial stringency and cost reduction could lead to a very different form of decentralisation from that envisaged in the preceding discussion.

6
Conclusions

As we come to the conclusion of our account, the media fascination with the Baby Peter case, and to a lesser extent the Sonnex case, is by no means exhausted. An additional factor in maintaining the focus was the publication by the government of the two Serious Case Reviews in the Baby Peter case (Department for Education 2010a, 2010b). The stated reason for the publication was to achieve 'closure' but, on the contrary, it has rather helped to keep the issue in the public focus, particularly given the fact that the high profile legal and official proceedings involving Sharon Shoesmith and Haringey social workers have only recently drawn to a conclusion. Shoesmith herself criticised the placing of the Serious Case Review in the public domain. In an interview in December 2010 she said:

> You can't have accountability models for one agency and different ones for another agency when they work together...Public accountability for me was police officers in my bedroom screwing down the windows. It was me being advised about my safety on the streets of London. It was being photographed on the tube and on buses. It was in my name and the names of my deputy, the service manager and the two social work staff as mugshots in a national newspaper. That's what social care professionals got as accountability. Public accountability was, I think, putting our lives at risk (Chandiramani 2010).

The final decision of the General Social Care Council Committee disciplinary panel on the two social workers involved with Baby

Peter, Maria Ward and her manager Gillie Christou, was not reached until the end of May 2010. The panel suspended them, Maria Ward for two months and Gillie Christou for four months for misconduct. However the panel argued that their removal from the social care register – which would have prevented their practicing again as social workers – would be a disproportionate reaction to any mistakes that were made in the management of Baby Peter case. Ward and Christou had also appealed against their dismissal by Haringey, taking the case to an employment tribunal, and this was not concluded until October 2010 with the failure of their appeal.

Interestingly far less media coverage was given to a third Haringey social worker, Sylvia Henry, who was successful in libel proceedings against Haringey for having publicised on its website the false allegation that she failed to raise concerns about Baby Peter. Haringey apologised unreservedly for the hurt and upset caused to Ms. Henry by misrepresentation of her role in the case and the compensation sum was kept confidential. The Henry case received far less media attention by comparison to the high levels of coverage discussing the fact that Ms. Ward and Ms. Christou retained their right to continue working in child protection. At the time of writing (December 2010) other court hearings are pending involving the consultant paediatrician accused of failing to spot Baby Peter's injuries a few days before his death and also legal action against the alleged chaotic state of affairs at the hospital where Baby Peter was taken to be examined (Bawden 2010).

Sharon Shoesmith, following the court case discussed in Chapter 4 above, continued to receive publicity when she appeared as the first expert witness before the House of Commons Education Committee hearings on Child Safeguarding in September 2010 (House of Commons Education Committee 2010). She opened her evidence with a statement:

> I really want to start by saying that there was never any doubt about how sorry I and everyone else at Haringey was about the murder of Peter Connelly – absolutely no doubt at all. To construct a narrative so simple, which told the public that Peter Connelly died because Haringey was uniquely weak, and that

sacking everyone from the director to the social workers meant that all would be well, was frankly absurd. The other story will be told eventually, but I want to start this morning by saying to you, Chair, that if you and your Committee members believe the narrative put to the public by some elements of the press and some politicians, we begin on different pages (House of Commons Education Committee 2010: 2).

There, briefly and succinctly, she re-stated the position she had held throughout the entire Baby Peter case. Continuing, she re-inforced the point which had been made by the Judge at her trial (see Chapter 4 above) that one of the effects of the negative public-ity was that 'the whole sector is now, in my view, motivated by a fear of failure and not the conditions for success'. She said:

The impact for children has been far-reaching...Since 2008, the number of children coming into care has increased by 30 percent ...The number of children subject to a child protection plan has doubled...Yet, sadly, this wider net seems to have had very little impact on the number of children who die. In the year that Peter died, sadly 54 other children also died...at the hands of their parents, close family members and wider family...Social work vacancies are high, fostering cannot meet demand, and almost a third of Directors of Children's Services left in just over a year (House of Commons Education Committee 2010: 2).

Her statements were, of course, extensively reported in the media. By contrast the Sonnex case gradually began to disappear below the horizon of media attention. Plans by the parents of Sonnex's victims Gabriel Ferez and Laurent Bonomo to sue Jack Straw have not, to date, materialised. Straw's apology may have been accepted by the parents (see Clements & Turnbull 2009). Meanwhile David Scott who, as already noted, found himself in an altogether different situ-ation from Sharon Shoesmith, reclaimed his voice mainly through a brief article in *Probation Journal* (Scott 2010). He has not, to date, been called to give evidence at any parliamentary or other inquiry. Despite his treatment at the hands of the Justice Secretary he can be thankful that he has not suffered the same experience as Sharon Shoesmith.

Social work and probation in a new cold climate

However, the obsession with the micro-details of these exceptional cases continues to act as a diversion from any popular engagement with the reality of the situation facing social work practitioners, probation officers, poor families and offenders, let alone the wider issues raised in this book. Some of the latter, such as the overwhelming power of the media and the normalisation of moral panic is well beyond the scope of this book for further detailed comment. It can be noted however that although the internet is hailed by many as an alternative popular voice, from both of our case studies, and in particular Baby Peter, we saw how powerful elements of the print media were able to use the internet for their own purposes as an extension and reinforcement of the moral panic originating in the print media. The *Sun*'s online petition (Haydon 2008) and the 5,000 members of the Facebook group in November 2008, which besides naming and shaming Connelly and Barker became a repository for various threats against them, serve as reminders that the internet can function as a device for the mobilisation of moral panic 'from below' every bit as much as a counterforce to moral panics orchestrated 'from above'.

Likewise political hysteria exemplified in political reactions to the Baby Peter and Sonnex cases reflected, I argued, quite fundamental changes in the relationship between the political elite and the public. Encapsulated in such phrases as 'the hollowing out of democracy' these changes reflect equally profound shifts in the structure of modern capitalist societies which, important as they are, are hardly going to be changed by a few recommendations from a book focused on probation and child protection.

A more legitimate starting point for a conclusion might be the problem of community decay and deprivation in large parts of our cities. This is, of course, related to the wider themes of moral panic and political hysteria. The lack of functioning community results, it has been argued, in a dependence on the media as a source of information and 'virtual community' through which is structured the relationship between the public and the political system. One of the themes of the politics chapter was the lack of a relationship between poor communities and the political elite through which the interests and concerns of ordinary people could be articulated and effectively represented and that this was the basis of government by media and what I termed the 'hysterical' relationship between communities, government and the media which was exemplified in the Baby Peter and Sonnex cases.

Community decay is also a central and widely recognised factor in the working of both social services and probation. It has been argued that the decline of community in deprived areas has been a factor militating against both social work engagement with community networks as caring resources and probation engagement with community as a resource for desistance. And as we shall see, recent initiatives launched by the new coalition government of Tories and Liberal Democrats which replaced 13 years of New Labour administrations in May 2010 do not appear to be aiming at an amelioration of community decay any time soon. Neither does the coalition appear to want to place significant additional resources in the hands of child protection social work or probation.

England as unique?

Before moving to a final conclusion it is useful to speculate as to how unique the developments we have described are to England, or the UK more generally, compared both with other parts of the European Union and with North America. Obviously a thorough discussion of the issue would take a book in itself but it would indeed seem strange in an increasingly interconnected world if there were not some similar developments, particularly in countries with a similar socio-economic and political structure to the UK. Certainly as regards the role of such cases as Sonnex and Baby Peter as vehicles for the mobilisation of public insecurities we have to look no further than Belgium and the well known case of Marc Dutroux.

Dutroux was a violent sex offender who, during 1995–6, kidnapped and murdered several young girls after locking them in his cellar. Two were rescued. The case provoked widespread criticism of the criminal justice system which had already been undergoing something of a legitimacy crisis (Fijnaut 2001). There is a strong similarity to the Sonnex case in that Dutroux was on parole licence at the time, having served three years of a 13 year sentence for a 1989 conviction for kidnapping and raping six teenage girls. He had been released for good behaviour – although against the advice of the public prosecutor.

Unlike the Sonnex case however the main focus of public and media criticism was the seeming incompetence of the police and judicial authorities in solving the murders, rather than on probation for ineffective supervision. Criticism of the police focused on the fact that the house containing the cellars where the girls were imprisoned had been searched several times and the police had even heard children crying. Suspicions that Dutroux was in fact being shielded by police were fuelled by the arrest of an inspector accused of being involved with Dutroux in a car-stealing ring (Fijnaut 2001: 237).

Further, in 1996 the examining magistrate in the case, Judge Jean-Marc Connerotte, who had a good public reputation, was removed from the case by the Supreme Court because he had attended a gathering to welcome home two of the survivors who had been eventually rescued from Dutroux's cellar that year. This triggered a demonstration in 1996 when over 300,000 people marched through the streets of Brussels to express outrage over the police blundering and the decision to remove Connerotte. More fundamentally, as in the English cases, the issue was the mobilisation of public fears and insecurities arising from social isolation and the erosion of community. As the French sociologist Georges Vigarello wrote:

> The sudden emphasis on rape-murder made possible the expression of collective forces that were elsewhere being eroded, gradually fragmented and diluted by a more individualistic society. This explains the obscure revenge of the demonstrators identifying with the victims, massed in a march of 300,000 people on 20th October in Brussels, denouncing a state that was 'powerless to protect its citizens, beginning with the weakest, the children'; rape-murder, once a news item, had become, by its very extremity, the ultimate political path (Vigarello 2001: 235).

The other difference is that although various senior criminal justice officials resigned during the course of the case this was not due to anything analogous to the actions of Jack Straw and Ed Balls. The resignations, of the commander of the State Police and the Minister of the Interior, were prompted by the fact that in 1998 Dutroux managed to escape custody from the court at Neufchateau where his trial was under way.

Because the shadow of incompetence hung over not probation officers and social workers but the entire police and judicial establishment, the government as a whole was seen as implicated and under an obligation to act to reform the system. One of the themes of this book has been the way that the Sonnex and Baby Peter cases diverted so much of the criticism to individual social workers and probation officers and their managers and, even when internal inquiries and Lord Laming's report were produced their orientation was basically that individuals had failed to do their jobs properly and that procedures needed to be tightened up.

Belgian governments had in fact, as Fijnaut (2001) notes, been preoccupied with reform of the criminal justice system since the 1980s and the Dutroux affair prompted the establishment of a further Parliamentary Commission on the subject. Again, the main focus was on such areas as removing the inefficiencies resulting from the fact that Belgium, like many continental European states, has several police forces with overlapping jurisdictions. A second theme was the training and auditing of examining magistrates and public prosecutors. Probation has a more marginal role in Belgium by comparison with England. Nevertheless it was also affected by general measures oriented to bringing the criminal justice agencies closer to the public. A diversity of 'para-judicial' services such as victim support, legal aid and also probation were brought together into local Houses of Justice co-ordinated by the Ministry of Justice in 1997 (Bauwens 2009: 259). Probation, moreover, was affected by the general civil service reforms announced in 1999 as part of the 'Copericus Plan' which introduced an orientation to efficiency and managerialism. The introduction of Business Process Re-engineering (Bauwens 2009: 260) can be compared with the type of risk management orientation described in the English context in earlier chapters.

What is interesting however from Bauwens' survey of probation officers in Brussels (Bauwens 2009) is that, unlike in England where probation officers have been transformed, frequently unwillingly, into 'Offender Managers' with an orientation away from rehabilitation towards public protection and the self-responsibilisation of the client for reform, in Belgium changes in organisation and working methods have:

> not taken probation officers away from the core values of social work...Moreover, most probation officers continue to demonstrate high levels of care and concern for their clients and often see themselves as professional 'social workers' working in the specialist setting of the criminal justice system...for probation officers accountability lies in the relationship of trust established between them and their client, crucial to the strategy of therapy, guidance and rehabilitation (Bauwens 2009: 264).

Belgium experienced a traumatic case involving child murder, public anxiety and the incompetence of the authorities which is at least equal to the English cases discussed in this book but, despite the introduction of comparable changes in working methods, probation has not as yet undergone the type of identity transformation (some would say identity crisis) that it has in England. Indeed Sonnex came after these changes had been implemented and reflected their impact whereas in Belgium changes came as a response to the Dutroux case and earlier system failures. In Belgium probation, as Bauwens notes, is probably closer to the Scottish system which retains a stronger connection with traditional social work values than the system in England and Wales.

Recent developments in Ireland tell a similar story in which the pace of change has been slower and there remains considerable faith in the rehabilitative paradigm and recent changes have been oriented towards the more effective implementation of rehabilitative goals so that 'traditional welfare practices, rather than being eclipsed, have been relegitimated through the new discourses of risk and protection' (Fitzgibbon et al. 2010: 170).

England, it appears, has gone further down the path to the transformation of probation from an orientation to the rehabilitation of offenders to the management of risk and the protection of the public from risky individuals who have to be kept under control.

The polar case of this risk management scenario is generally cited as the United States where for sociologists such as Wacquant the penal system has largely degenerated into a system for warehousing the poor (Wacquant 2007, 2009) due to the development of a large fragmented permanently unemployed section of the working class in the context of a dismembering of the welfare state. More generally for over a decade the US has been a theoretical powerhouse for the development of the thesis that rehabilitation has been replaced by the management of risk groups (Feeley & Simon 1992, 1994; Simon 2007).

In such a context probation becomes simply a form of warehousing outside the walls of the prison: a containment strategy for the marginalised and permanently unemployed, with the implication that any sort of therapeutic or personal relationship between probation/parole officer and client is largely irrelevant. You do not have to know anything about people in order to warehouse them. In this context the study by Mona Lynch (2000) of the transition of the Californian parole system from rehabilitation to managing risk is significant, a process which she traces back to as early as the beginning of the 1980s. She argues that although the official 'mission statement' of the parole service still stresses rehabilitation this has largely been seen as a responsibility of the clients themselves and that in fact the priorities of the agency have 'shifted in large part to managing, controlling and containing the risk posed by the clientele in the most effective and least politically risky manner' (Lynch 2000: 44).

In many respects the English model appears closer to this. By comparison with countries geographically closer such as Belgium, Scotland and Ireland, England appears to be, in policy terms, somewhere in Mid-Atlantic.

Recent policy developments in England and Wales

To return, in conclusion, to the present situation in England and Wales, there are of course some policy changes introduced by the new coalition government that can be welcomed. In the area of child protection Liz Davies, writing in the last months of the New Labour administration, expressed support for the proposed abolition of the intrusive registration of all children. 'The Tories have promised to abolish the huge children's database and restore a slimmed down Child Protection Register for genuinely at-risk children. I cannot wait' (Davies 2009). As noted in Chapter 4, the closure of the

ContactPoint database was one of the early actions of the new government. A further promising sign is the appointment in June 2010 of one of the strongest academic critics of the tick-box culture, Eileen Munro, to conduct an independent review of children's social work and frontline child protection practice. Her preliminary overview, published in October 2010 (the full report is expected in March 2011), showed a clear recognition of some of the problems currently facing child protection and was in line with her criticisms of the tick-box culture and computerised systems such as the Integrated Children's System (ICS):

> A dominant theme in the criticisms of current practice is the skew in priorities that has developed between the demands of the management and inspection processes and professionals' ability to exercise their professional judgment and act in the best interests of the child. This has led to an over-standardised system that cannot respond adequately to the varied range of children's needs (Munro 2010b: 5).

Following Lord Laming's 2009 report Ed Balls announced a £58m funding package some of which would be devoted to easing pressures on front line social work while other parts of the package would fund 200 university places from September 2011 to attract graduates into social work and a new Advanced Social Work Professional Status programme to help experienced social workers remain in front line work. However, as noted in Chapter 4, it is not clear how far such an initiative will survive £670m cuts in children's services.

In the criminal justice area the new Justice Secretary, Ken Clarke, has moved swiftly to signal a change of direction. A minister in his department, Crispin Blunt, speaking to the Probation Association in September 2010, said that it was the Government's intention to liberate probation from the 'target culture':

> Diverting you and your people into becoming data inputters is a shocking waste of your professional value. We know your staff are spending far too much time on paperwork rather than face-to-face contact with offenders. We will examine all ways of changing that (Probation Association 2010).

Privatising rehabilitation

Although not as extensive as the new moves in child protection – there is no academic expert with a brief to re-evaluate methods of work – the sentiments here seem similar. In December 2010 the Green Paper on criminal justice was published: *Breaking the Cycle: Effective Punishment, Rehabilitation and Sentencing of Offenders* (Ministry of Justice 2010) inviting responses from interested parties by March 2011. As regards probation, an important theme is the aim to reduce re-offending rates particularly among young offenders through measures which include a re-emphasis on rehabilitation:

> The fundamental failing of policy has been the lack of a firm focus on reform and rehabilitation, so that most criminals continue to commit more crimes against more victims once they are released back onto the streets...We will pilot at least six new rehabilitation programmes, delivered on a payment by results basis. Providers will be paid to reduce reoffending, funded in the long run by the savings to the taxpayer that this new approach is expected to generate. We expect that independent providers, backed up by ethical investment, will support the early stages of this rehabilitation revolution (Ministry of Justice 2010: 1).

At a first reading this might be taken as a welcome signal to probation officers that a move away from the overwhelming centrality of tick-box risk assessment systems in offender management and the devotion of more time and resources to the processes which, as noted in previous chapters, research indicates to be the most viable strategies for offender rehabilitation, is imminent. There is a widespread recognition of the importance of getting the ex-offender into employment as part of the process of rehabilitation and desistance. It is recognised that offenders having served a custodial sentence may have problems finding a job and so new employer-led training initiatives are promised as well as 'working prisons' in which inmates do a 'full working week'. For those being released from prison or serving community sentences it is recognised that:

> If offenders are to become law-abiding citizens and contribute to society then they will need to find a job and somewhere to live,

otherwise the effectiveness of other rehabilitation work can be lost (Ministry of Justice 2010: 32).

Such a move would certainly meet with the approval of practitioners who have laboured to retain, despite the new approaches to training outlined in the previous chapter, an orientation to the importance of a relationship with the offender as the starting point for getting the offender out of crime:

> Bring professionalism back. I don't know how the new training will maintain that, the motivation over the 18 months to three years training particularly as it's distance learning and they have a high caseload. I just cannot see it. They're being used as a resource and their training needs seem to be ignored. You want to have that moment to sit back and reflect. During my training I was allowed to reflect. I think the new training needs to be scrapped . There was a lot to be said for our face-to-face training but I believe if people cannot muster it they should be allowed to fail. I sound quite pessimistic really. I do love probation. *Sophie – Probation Officer*

> Supervision should not be about targets and outputs but about analysis of case materials to enhance practice. Training should encourage the ability to build relationships and the current move to all distance learning will not help develop these skills. On a positive note I think the need for more traditional super-vision has been recognised by London probation; however, I am concerned that many of the SPOs in post are audit lead and trained, and do not have the skills set to manage in this way. Although, I personally have been lucky enough to be managed by experienced seniors throughout my career. *Damien – Probation Officer*

> I would like training to emphasise working with offenders more closely, placements in hostels upfront with offenders. They may lose some of their fear and remember that offenders are just people. I would like a lot more emphasis on interviewing skills and setting the technologies around that. Maybe even bringing back experience of group work...greater contact with offenders so

that they are recognised as members of society. The idea of social inclusion. To keep engaging with people and not feel they are outside or other than you. Better interview skills and more trust. More time which would pay dividends. *Marvin – Probation Manager*

Such comments have for their support the desistance literature and other academic work, in social work and mental health, which supports the importance of the working relationships professionals build with their clients in order to be able to influence the behaviour of the latter in a positive and harm reducing way. It would be wrong for the new government and private and voluntary organisations to dismiss public sector professionals as a defeated force. Strong voices of optimism still remain:

> taking the evidence seriously about what helps offenders to desist from their offending careers, actually takes the Service back to its traditional concerns with working with the individual in the context of their family and wider community relationships and supports...working with people, developing their personal capacity and enhancing their social capital – the resources they can utilize in their own rehabilitation – supported by evidence-based interventions is ultimately a human and moral enterprise. Returning offenders to the status of responsible citizens accepted and integrated within their own communities ultimately offers the public much greater safety than the expensive incarceration in a burgeoning prison population that has been a key motif and consequence of New Labour policies (Burke & Collett 2010: 244).

However, the re-emphasis on rehabilitation in Ken Clarke's Green Paper is accompanied by a strong commitment to 'payment by results' and an emphasis on the role of the voluntary and private sectors which are seen as making a significant, if not the major, contribution to the 'rehabilitation revolution'.

> Our decentralising approach will mean a move away from centrally controlled services dominated by the public sector, towards a more competitive system that draws on the knowledge,

expertise and innovation of a much broader set of organisations from all sectors (Ministry of Justice 2010: 8).

Probation Trusts will be given more autonomy in how they manage themselves so that they can compete with other agencies in payment by results.

> We will explore the scope for new business models that can deliver better services, reduce costs, and enable partnership with the communities in which local agencies work...This will support the transition of the public probation service towards a payment by results model (Ministry of Justice 2010: 47).

It must be recognised that it was New Labour that opened the door to private providers in probation. The Carter Report (Home Office 2003), on the basis of which probation was amalgamated with the Prison Service to form the National Offender Management Service (NOMS), proposed that NOMS would embrace what Carter termed 'contestability', that is the commissioning of various resources for offender management from private and voluntary as well as public sector agencies, establishing a market in offender-related services. This in effect laid the basis for the initiatives of the coalition government.

> Although the report was somewhat sketchy in terms of how contestability would be implemented, it was likely that Probation Areas would become providers and would have to bid for contracts against the private, voluntary and community sectors to deliver services (many of which it already held statutory responsibility for). Contestability thus ushered in a potentially different relationship between the Probation Service and the voluntary sector with a greater emphasis on competition than the traditional partnership approach (Burke & Collett 2010: 236).

So the policies announced by the new coalition government are by no means discontinuous with those of New Labour. They face, nevertheless, the problem that they are to be implemented under the worst possible combination of circumstances: cuts in funding across public sector agencies and economic recession. Chief

Probation Officers in England and Wales recently voiced their concerns about their ability to cope with a move away from short-term custodial sentences towards more community-based sentences as set out in the Green Paper. In a survey of 20 of the 35 Chief Officers only three thought their service 'had the capacity to cope effectively with a move away from short custodial sentences to more community-based sentences and all 20 expected their budgets to be cut in the next two years' (BBC News 2010b). Meanwhile current (October 2010) plans for spending reductions across the public sector are expected to result in 14,000 job losses at the Ministry of Justice with a possible 9,940 of these being in NOMS (Winnett & Porter 2010).

Substantial cuts in core probation services are likely to result in an increased pressure for serious offenders to find their way to supervision by the various outsourced services which will, it seems reasonable to assume, take over much of the work currently undertaken by less skilled Probation Service Officers. There is of course no reason why, in principle, private and voluntary sector organisations should not employ well-trained practitioners implementing sophisticated rehabilitation strategies.

However, an important concern here is that the monitoring of practitioner standards and skills, difficult enough in a single national probation service, would be immeasurably harder under conditions of a medley of different providers being chosen less because of their skill base and experience than because they offer the cheapest in terms of contract. Part of the motive for privatisation is undoubtedly cost reduction. Those private sector organisations which already have considerable involvement in public sector and criminal justice work such as Group 4 Security are explicitly competing for government contracts on the basis of cost reduction. In November 2010 Group 4 was reported as signing a 'memorandum of understanding' with the government:

> G4S said it had signed a memorandum of understanding with ministers setting out £10 million of savings 'through specifica-tion amendments on existing contracts'. Alison Flynn for G4S said the deal would mean 'efficiency savings' on things such as maintenance regimes and cleaning, amid signs of the Govern-ment's success at hammering down contract costs with private

suppliers...G4S added that it believed there are 'a number of areas where the private sector can deliver further cost savings to the Government' and earmarked the operation of police custody suites, the Welfare to Work programme, and the probation service as areas where it could "grow its market share" (Tobin 2010).

The idea of Group 4 or similar organisations growing their market share in probation through efficiency savings and at the same time investing in the training and employment of practitioners skilled in rehabilitation is hardly credible. Indeed there are indications that the tendency to deskilling, which has been underway for some time in probation in the form of PSOs who handle lower risk offenders (see Chapter 5), would be accentuated as part of cost saving. According to one recent press report:

> A "dads' army" of former soldiers would run community service programmes for offenders under a radical cost-cutting privat- isation plan that has shocked unions. Napo, which represents probation staff, said it was alarmed to learn the plan had been discussed at a meeting between the prisons minister, Crispin Blunt, probation representatives and two officials from the National Offender Management Service this month. Under the plan, pri- vate companies bidding for contracts to run the unpaid work programmes would be asked to recruit former non-commissioned officers – servicemen who have worked their way up through the ranks – to help run them (Doward 2010).

The notion that unqualified personnel are capable of monitoring and supervising offenders not just with regard to the performing of unpaid work elements of community sentences but in the crucial area of motivating offenders to desist from crime – requiring skills that experienced probation officers take years to acquire – is fanciful. The ability to provide adequate pro-social modelling for offenders who often have experienced authority in a negative and challenging way and skilfully to engage with anti-authoritarian attitudes and challenging behaviour in order to elicit positive change and reduce offending cannot be provided on the cheap. The danger is that a focus on desistance will give way to simple supervision and control and community punishment will assimilate to a variety of 'ware- housing the poor' (Wacquant 2009).

So there is a basic contradiction: if the government is serious about rehabilitation then it needs to equip the personnel of the voluntary and private sector with the type of mentoring and person-to-person skills necessary to motivate often tragic individuals at key turning points in their lives. One has only to imagine someone like Sonnex being managed by a private security company. This is not as fanciful as it might seem because, although those classified as high risk offenders on the basis of systems such as OASys may remain in the hands of skilled offender managers (albeit with high case-loads entirely of serious offenders), Sonnex, it will be remembered, had the wrong risk classification. Such mis-classifications are more, rather than less, likely where there are a number of different supervising agencies involved. More importantly, as noted already (see Chapter 5), risk levels can change and low risk offenders can get into the situational contexts in which they commit serious further offences.

A further area of problems with the new proposed arrangements concerns the practical working of 'payment by results'. This might seem to involve very simple measurements: which voluntary or private sector agency achieves the best results in terms of a minimisation of rates of re-offending? Those addicted to free-market solutions to social provision may argue that the agencies competing to achieve best results would have an incentive to train their operatives to become skilled probation officers. This however presupposes at the very least that the actual results achieved by an agency can be easily measured. The attempt to devise accurate monitoring may lead to a return of the target culture by the back door. David Boyle of the New Economics Foundation outlined the problems which lie ahead. Payment by results:

> makes logical sense, and it can sometimes be possible if the measures are simple – have the ex-prisoners reoffended or not? Have the jobseekers found work? The problem is that outcomes are not simple. Working out exactly which contractor is responsible for which outcome is almost impossible. The really worthwhile outcomes can't be measured anyway – have the prisoners stayed out of trouble because they are out of their heads on drugs? Have contractors been cherry picking their candidates? And so the regulations begin to mount, the inspectors loom, and the actual results paid for become narrower and more closely defined. It also

means that small contractors will either have to wait for months or years to be paid, or they will be paid on the basis of proxies for outcomes – narrower and more immediate (Boyle 2010).

The final, and probably the most important, factor working against the success of whatever mix of privatised supervision and community sentencing emerges as part of government criminal justice policy during 2011 is the effect of economic recession and the general shift of social policy in the direction of workfare. The latter drift has been going on for some decades and was well entrenched under New Labour:

> Labour market policies, referred to as welfare to work policies, have been based on a supply-side policy paradigm according to which economic inactivity and unemployment are not caused by a lack of demand, but by the individual characteristics of the economically inactive. Interestingly, the recession and the subsequent increase in unemployment, from about 6% prior to the recession to 8% in May 2010, did not shake the faith in this supply side paradigm. As a result, there is a strong cross party consensus in favour of workfare schemes, with only minimal disagreements between the Labour and the Conservative Party (Daguerre 2010: 1).

The coalition government have simply toughened up this approach with the plan to simplify benefit entitlements and additional sanctions for refusing 'reasonable' offers of employment in the form of possible loss of benefits for up to three years. As noted in Chapter 3, this 'supply-side policy paradigm' impacts directly on services like probation in that clients have to embrace desistance and the appropriate job-seeking behaviour as a pre-requisite to securing the employment which may get them out of crime (Fitzgibbon & Lea 2010). Meanwhile community sentences involving unpaid work – with which Ken Clarke wants to replace many short-term custodial sentences – are facing a declining supply of opportunities. As Harry Fletcher of the National Association of Probation Officers (NAPO) recently emphasised:

> Currently the Probation Service in England and Wales is finding it somewhat difficult to find placements for the 50,000 individuals a year who are sentenced to unpaid work and the government is

likely to experience severe difficulty in finding suitable additional placements for what could be several hundred thousand individuals (Fletcher 2010: 5).

Fletcher goes on to point out that the population serving community sentences under probation supervision are likely to merge with the population performing compulsory work as a condition of receiving benefits:

> a significant proportion of those in receipt of long term job seekers allowance will be known to Probation and will have problems with drugs and alcohol and lead chaotic lifestyles and have little hope of finding work. Also, if the proposal goes ahead, it will make participation in unpaid work as a condition of receiving benefits no different from criminal supervision under the auspices of a court order. This will undermine the value of such supervision (Fletcher 2010: 5).

As the two populations merge, social welfare and criminal justice increasingly become different branches of the same apparatus for the punishment of the poor, the visitation of the consequences of the economic and financial crisis upon the shoulders of those who played no part in its genesis.

The new minimal state

While a promising re-orientation of probation towards rehabilitation threatens to be undermined by privatisation, target culture and economic recession, so the Munro reforms in child protection are likely to meet similar obstacles. Of course Munro's full report is not due until March 2011 but any stress on the necessity for the professional judgement of the frontline practitioner to be focused on the child at risk and his or her environment rather than the computer screen will encounter familiar pressures working in the opposite direction. Like the probation officers who want to re-emphasise the relationship with the client, the social workers interviewed wanted to get away from the tick-box culture and think properly about their work.

> I try to do good supervision but I am conscious through my own time restrictions, I do find that you can get into have you done

this, have you done that, but we need to put a time aside to really think properly about cases. The pressures of the job, the awful IT systems we have that force us to work in a kind of certain way. They enforce this tick-box culture. And you have to try and get away from that because that's dangerous...We're always trying to do it the other way round: trying to make IT work for the way we are trying to work. But it's difficult. In terms of training I don't want to give the picture that there are all these terrible social workers, I think there are some tremendous social workers out there. But what I'd like to see the profession doing is saying 'yes there is a high bar', be seen as a profession people value. *Pippa – Social Work Manager*

To do this job it's not a tick box job and if it does become a tick-box job that's when you should stop doing it. You have to have a dynamism especially when you're working with families that are going to try and hoodwink you. Ultimately you end up with families in an abusive situation and you've got to go in there with a really dynamic thinking, what is really going on: who is that, what does this mean? You have to think about child development, someone's mental state, family dynamics, community dynamics, it's such a complex situation. Going into a family home you remember how intense it is to think about what's really going on there. Trying to make an accurate assessment and trying to pull together all the information. It's complicated and difficult stuff and it's demanding and requires demanding training in order to understand the kind of work that they're getting into. But during training some of it is so dumbed down, some of the training I did was really challenging good stuff (I did the diploma in social work), but there was no consistency, in terms of the standard. *Kristy – Social Worker*

Like probation, social work is faced with a combination of cuts in spending and a government enthusiasm for the role of the private and voluntary sectors. The latter is celebrated by Prime Minister David Cameron as part of a fundamental shift which he sees as a socially inclusive 'Big Society'. In a speech in July 2010 he outlined the philosophy of a 'huge culture change':

The Big Society is about a huge culture change...where people, in their everyday lives, in their homes, in their neighbourhoods, in their workplace...don't always turn to officials, local authorities or central government for answers to the problems they face...but instead feel both free and powerful enough to help themselves and their own communities. It's about people setting up great new schools. Businesses helping people getting trained for work. Charities working to rehabilitate offenders (Cameron 2010).

To this can be added the prospect of the introduction of volunteers to supplement the work of frontline child protection officers. Tim Loughton, Ed Ball's successor as Children's Minister, claimed this as an example of the 'Big Society' in action. Praising a child protection scheme running in the London Borough of Bromley, organised by the private charity, Community Service Volunteers (CSV), he said:

"You have volunteers working alongside professional social workers, on child protection cases. They have had a fantastic success...I don't see why it couldn't apply everywhere...At a time when the number of children going into care is still rising as an after-effect of the Baby Peter case, and when the amount of money councils have available to spend on them is diminishing", Loughton said, "across the piste we have got to do more for less" (Gentleman 2010).

The attitude of social worker professional bodies is generally – as has been the case for some years – to welcome such voluntary input. Pilot projects involving volunteers giving parenting help to the families of children at risk of neglect were established by CSV in 2005 and recent research confirms the useful role these can play (Tunstill 2007; Valios 2010). However, this activity is not a substitute for close supervision of children at risk by professional social workers. Tim Loughton's 'discovery' of such schemes under conditions in which, to use his words, 'we have got to do more for less', that is under conditions of massive cuts in local authority spending conveniently legitimised by reference to a 'Big Society' of volunteers, suggests the likelihood that children at risk of serious neglect will end up in the hands of unskilled volunteers, just as in probation serious offenders may end up being managed by an untrained private sector. Such developments would of course work completely against the spirit of the Munro review which aims to find ways of enabling professional trained social workers to spend more time working with families at risk. These dangers were the theme of a recent article in the *Guardian* newspaper signed by a group of academics and practitioners, including this author.

> The proposed implementation [*of child protection volunteers*] more widely in the UK is prompted not by the safety of children but by a strategy steered by cuts in services using unqualified and minimally trained volunteers to visit children with complex protection needs. The potential for subjecting these volunteers to risk, both physical and emotional, is significant. But more concerning is that volunteers may place vulnerable children at greater risk of harm, however good their intentions, merely by their inexperience and lack of accountability.
>
> Projects and services that depend on the hard work of volunteers have been successfully collaborating with statutory children's services for many years. Proactive child protection depends on the active involvement of communities in ensuring children are safe from harm. This lay involvement, however, risks becoming, at a time of ever-reducing welfare services, a substitute for the professional expertise that vulnerable, abused children are entitled to (Lebloch & Beresford 2010).

Meanwhile professional social workers, whatever the outcome of the Munro review, are left to contemplate a future of diminishing resources.

> I think it's a real worry about the amount of money we have to save and where it's going to come from and what the impact is on the front line services. They may not cut the number of child protection social workers but other things that are in place that support families and what we do potentially could be cut. And the resources we have for the work with the families will also potentially be affected. I think we are quite fortunate in that we do still have resources to work with clients but I know in lots of local authorities they don't have the same resources. It's increasingly difficult even here to get funding for all kinds of things agreed. I think that's only going to get worse. *Emma – Social Work Manager*

In a few short months it has become clear that the ideological invocation of the Big Society is actually obscuring a war against the poor. Massive reductions in public spending may arguably be a response to the global economic recession that any government would have to contemplate and New Labour had certainly planned for cuts but, from the point of view of social services and criminal justice, precisely which social strata feel the impact of the cuts is of the utmost importance. For at least some of the measures implemented so far the answer appears to be very straightforward: the poor. Precisely those social groups most at risk of the issues discussed in this book are the apparent targets of stringent cuts in public spending.

For those living in rented accommodation and in receipt of housing benefits reforms announced in June 2010 will involve caps on the level of benefits. In the absence of parallel controls on the level of housing rents or the building of more affordable housing, the caps may well make some large conurbations simply too expensive as places to live for poor people. Calculations by the Chartered Institute of Housing indicate that:

> the effect of the CPI cap will be to break the link between the help tenants receive with their housing costs and the actual rent they pay. At this point it can no longer be said that housing benefit will be meeting its central policy objective: to ensure that reasonably priced accommodation is available to all households regardless of their income (Chartered Institute of Housing 2010: 4).

The result is likely to be large numbers of poor families forced to move out of London and the South East and relocate in the North where unemployment is higher. The combination of the benefit changes with other tax changes will be further economic and social marginalisation of the poor, in particular a substantial increase in child poverty. Research by The Institute for Fiscal Studies suggests that:

> The Government's tax and benefit reforms [will] act to increase absolute poverty in 2013–14 by about 300,000 children, about 200,000 working-age parents and about 300,000 working-age adults without children, and [will] increase relative poverty in 2013–14 by about 200,000 children, about 200,000 working-age

parents and about 200,000 working age adults without children (Institute for Fiscal Studies 2010: 2).

A third example is the impact of recent cuts in grants to Local Government in which:

> deprived inner-city areas of London and large cities in the north are facing the most drastic reductions of up to 8.9% this year alone, with the shires and county councils relatively protected by their burgeoning council tax revenue. The Local Government Association labelled the cuts the "toughest in living memory" (Curtis 2010).

These are merely examples which give the flavour of the new policy agenda. The shift seems to be away from the surveillance and controlling state favoured by New Labour towards the minimal state of American-inspired neo-liberalism in which large areas of welfare and criminal justice services are privatised or left to communities to provide themselves on a voluntary basis. Some will be able to do this but for many large desolated and fragmented communities that are unable to cope the future looks bleak indeed. Poor families with children, unstable marriages or short-term cohabitees, ex-offenders seeking a route out of crime will all find new obstacles to their desire for stable lives (see Farrall et al. 2010).

At the same time I have noted a continued concern on the part of practitioners in both probation and child protection to maintain and develop close work with their respective client groups. There is a desire to move away from a one-dimensional orientation to risk management and to develop multi-dimensional relationships with offenders to help them get back into a normal social life and with the families of children at risk of neglect to help them out of isolation and child abuse: desires which, in the area of child protection at least, may well be legitimised by the government's own sponsored policy review due to report in Spring 2011. For both groups of practitioners the building of strong communities is a central part of the process of turning offenders away from crime and with breaking down the isolation of children at risk of abuse. A political clash between the privatisation and neo-liberal orientations of the Coalition government and the needs of professionals working in probation and child protection seems therefore inevitable.

Bibliography

Aarvold, C., Hill, D. & Newton, G. (1973). *Report on the Review of Procedures into the Discharge of Psychiatric Patients Subject to Special Restrictions (Cmnd 5191)*. London: HMSO.

Aas, K.F. (2004). 'From narrative to database: Technological change and penal culture'. *Punishment and Society*, 6, 379–393.

Action for Children (2009). 'Neglect statistics'. Retrieved 26th October 2010, from http://www.actionforchildren.org.uk/content/642/Neglect-statistics

Allan, G. (1983). 'Informal networks of care: Issues raised by Barclay'. *British Journal of Social Work*, 13, 417–433.

Allen, V. & Fernandez, C. (2008, 12th November). 'Treated like a dog, used as a punch bag: Life and death of a baby boy called "Smiley"'. *Daily Mail*.

Altheide, D. (2002). *Creating Fear: News and the Construction of Crisis*. New York: Transaction.

Altheide, D. (2009). 'Moral panic: From sociological concept to public discourse'. *Crime Media Culture*, 5(1), 80–99.

Annison, J. (2007). 'A gendered review of change within the probation service'. *The Howard Journal of Criminal Justice*, 46(2), 145–161.

Annison, J., Eadie, T. & Knight, C. (2008). 'People first: Probation officer perspectives on probation work'. *Probation Journal*, 55(3), 259–271.

Ansbro, M. (2006). 'What can we learn from Serious Incident Reports'. *Probation Journal*, 53(1), 57–70.

Ansbro, M. (2008). 'Using attachment theory with offenders'. *Probation Journal*, 55(3), 231–244.

Atkins, H. (2007). 'Memories of Whitehawk in the 1950s'. Retrieved 25th October 2010, from http://www.mybrightonandhove.org.uk/page_id__8007_ path__0p114p462p1242p.aspx

Bailey, R. & Brake, M. (1975). *Radical Social Work*. London: Hodder & Stoughton.

Barclay Report (1982). *Social Workers: Their Role and Tasks*. London: Bedford Square Press.

Barry, M. (2007). 'Listening and learning: The reciprocal relationship between worker and client'. *Probation Journal*, 54(4), 407–422.

Batty, D. (2008, 22nd May). 'Council failed girl who died in neglect case, says MP'. *The Guardian*.

Bauman, Z. (1998). *Work, Consumerism and the New Poor*. Buckingham: Open University Press.

Bauman, Z. (2007). *Consuming Life*. Cambridge: Polity.

Bauwens, A. (2009). 'Probation officers' perspectives on recent Belgian changes in the probation service'. *Probation Journal*, 56(3), 257–268.

Bawden, A. (2010, 20th September). 'Doctor and social workers take legal action over Baby P case'. *The Guardian*.

BBC News (2008, 7th November). 'Child death review shows failures'. Retrieved 26th October 2010, from http://news.bbc.co.uk/1/hi/england/south_york-shire/7716723.stm

BBC News (2010a, 1st April 2010). 'Ofsted changed Shoesmith report'. Retrieved 13th November 2010, from http://news.bbc.co.uk/1/hi/education/8599616.stm

BBC News (2010b, 31st August). 'Probation chiefs' "concern" over community sentences'. Retrieved 13th December, from http://www.bbc.co.uk/news/uk-11146517

BBC Today (2009). 'Child protection reforms "part of the problem"'. Retrieved 21st November 2010, from http://news.bbc.co.uk/today/hi/today/newsid_7939000/7939043.stm

Benjamin, A. (2008, 11th November). 'Baby P case: Child protection experts' responses'. *Guardian*. Retrieved from http://www.guardian.co.uk/society/2008/nov/11/baby-p-child-protection

Berg, S. (2010, 10th June). 'New social work model brings hope'. *BBC News*.

Bird, S. (2009, 5th June). 'Dano Sonnex: A career criminal determined to live up to family name'. *The Times*.

Bird, S. & Ford, R. (2009, 5th June). 'Blunders revealed as Dano Sonnex and Nigel Farmer guilty of French student murders'. *The Times*.

Bowden, P. (1996). 'Graham Young (1947–90); the St Albans poisoner: His life and times'. *Criminal Behaviour and Mental Health*, 6(S1), 17–24.

Boyle, D. (2010, 8th October). 'Target culture: Back from the dead'. *The Guardian*.

Broadhurst, K., Hall, C., Wastell, D., White, S. & Pithouse, A. (2010). 'Risk, instrumentalism and the humane project – identifying the informal logics of risk management in children's statutory services'. *British Journal of Social Work*, 40(4), 1046–1064.

Brogden, M. (1982). *The Police: Autonomy and Consent*. London: Academic Press.

Burke, L. (2009). 'A broken profession or a broken society?' *Probation Journal*, 56(1), 5–8.

Burke, L. (2009). 'A collective failure?' *Probation Journal*, 56(3), 219–223.

Burke, L. (2010). 'Nudging not forcing'. *Probation Journal*, 57(4), 363–367.

Burke, L. & Collett, S. (2010). 'People are not things: What New Labour has done to probation'. *Probation Journal*, 57(3), 232–249.

Burke, R. (1996). *The History of Child Protection in Britain: A Theoretical Reformulation*. Leicester: Scarman Centre.

Burnett, R. (2004). 'One-to-one ways of promoting desistance: In search of an evidence base'. In R. Burnett & C. Roberts (eds), *What Works in Probation and Youth Justice: Developing evidence based practice*. Devon: Willan Publishing.

Burnett, R. & Maruna, S. (2006). 'The kindness of prisoners: Strengths-based resettlement in theory and in action'. *Criminology and Criminal Justice*, 6(1), 83–106.

Burton, F. & Carlen, P. (1979). *Official Discourse: On Discourse Analysis, Government Publications, Ideology and the State*. London: Routledge and Kegan Paul.

Burton, J. & van den Broek, D. (2009). 'Accountable and countable: Information management systems and the bureaucratization of social work'. *British Journal of Social Work, 39*(7), 1326–1342.

Butler, I. & Drakeford, M. (2008). 'Booing or cheering? Ambiguity in the construction of victimhood in the case of Maria Colwell'. *Crime, Media, Culture, 4*(3), 367–385.

Cameron, D. (2010, 19th July). 'Big society speech: Transcript of a speech by the Prime Minister on the big society', 19th July 2010. Retrieved 13th November, from http://www.number10.gov.uk/news/speeches-and-transcripts/2010/07/big-society-speech-53572

Carvel, J. (2008, 13th November). 'Social worker chiefs call for an end to demonisation of their colleagues'. *The Guardian.*

Caulkin, S. (2008, 23rd November). 'Blame bureaucrats and systems for Baby P's fate'. *The Observer.*

Chandiramani, R. (2010, 7th December). 'The Shoesmith interview: "I haven't been able to move on at all"'. *Children & Young People Now.* Retrieved from http://www.cypnow.co.uk/inDepth/1045184

Chartered Institute of Housing (2010). *Impact of Housing Benefit Reforms – November 2010.* Cambridge: Chartered Institute of Housing.

Chibnall, S. (1977). *Law and Order News.* London: Tavistock.

Chief Secretary to the Treasury (2003). *Every Child Matters. (Cm 5860).* London: TSO.

Clements, J. & Turnbull, G. (2009, 5th June). 'French student murders: Victims parents to sue after authority blunders left killer free'. *The Mirror.*

Clements, J. & Shaw, A. (2008, 12th November). 'Baby P. trial: Two convicted of toddlers torture death'. *Daily Mirror.*

Cohen, S. (1972). *Folk Devils and Moral Panics: The Creation of the Mods and Rockers.* London: MacGibbon and Kee.

Cohen, S. & Young, J. (1981). *The Manufacture of News: Deviance, Social Problems and the Mass Media* London: Constable.

Collins, S., Coffey, M. & Cowe, F. (2009). 'Stress, support and well-being as perceived by probation trainees'. *Probation Journal, 56*(3), 238–256.

Community Care (1974, 11th September). 'The Maria Colwell Report: What the papers had to say'. *Community Care.*

Cooper, A., Hetherington, R. & Katz, I. (2003). *The Risk Factor – Reforming the child protection system.* London: Demos.

Craissati, J. & Sindall, O. (2009). 'Serious further offences: An exploration of risk and typologies'. *Probation Journal, 56*, 9–27.

Critcher, C. (2009). 'Widening the focus: Moral panics as moral regulation'. *British Journal of Criminology, 49*(1), 17–34.

Cunningham, J. (1973, 8th December). 'The buck doesn't stop with Maria'. *The Guardian.*

Curtis, P. (2010, 13th December). 'Poorest councils will face biggest cuts'. *The Guardian.*

Daguerre, A. (2010). *Welfare to Work Policies in the UK: The Workfare Consensus.* Paris: CNRS.

Daily Mail Reporter (2008, 16th November). 'Teenager reveals full horror of shocking ordeal suffered by Baby P at the hands of his tormentors'. *Daily Mail*.

Daily Mail Comment (2009, 4th June). 'National shame of our justice system'. *Daily Mail*.

Davies, L. (2009, 11th May). 'Why there will soon be a new Baby P scandal'. *Daily Mail*.

Davies, L. (2010). *Protecting Children – A Critical Contribution to Policy and Practice Development* (unpublished PhD thesis). London: London Metropolitan University.

Davies, L. & Duckett, N. (2008). *Proactive Child Protection and Social Work*. Exeter: Learning Matters.

Davies, N. (1997). *Dark Heart: The Shocking Truth About Hidden Britain*. London: Chatto and Windus.

Department for Children Schools and Families (2010). 'Every child matters: ContactPoint'. Retrieved 22nd November 2010, from http://www.dcsf. gov. uk/everychildmatters/strategy/deliveringservices1/contactpoint/contact-point/

Department for Education (2010a). *Haringey Local Safeguarding Children Board Serious Case Review 'Child A' November 2008*. London: Department for Education.

Department for Education (2010b). *Haringey Local Safeguarding Children Board Serious Case Review 'Child A' March 2009*. London: Department for Education.

Dorling, D., Rigby, J. & Wheeler, B. (2007). *Poverty, Wealth and Place in Britain, 1968 to 2005*. Bristol: Policy Press.

Dorling, D., Vickers, D., Thomas, B., Pritchard, J. & Ballas, D. (2008). *Changing UK: The Way We Live Now*. Sheffield: Social and Spatial Inequalities (SASI) group, Department of Geography, University of Sheffield.

Doward, J. (2010, 19th September). 'Former soldiers could make community service tougher for offenders'. *The Guardian*.

Doward, J., Hinsliff, G., McVeigh, T. & Townsend, M. (2008, 16th November). 'Why children are left to die beyond help's reach'. *The Observer*.

Downes, D. & Morgan, R. (1997). 'Dumping the "hostages to fortune"? The politics of law and order in post-war Britain'. In M. Maguire, R. Morgan & R. Reiner (eds), *The Oxford Handbook of Criminology*. Oxford: Oxford University Press.

Drake, M. (2008, 14th November). 'Ascot and luxury foreign trips – a portrait of Haringey's head of children's services'. *Daily Mail*.

Drakeford, M. & Butler, I. (2010). 'Familial homicide and social work'. *British Journal of Social Work*, *40*, 1419–1433.

Farrall, S. (2004). 'Supervision, motivation and social context: What matters most when probationers desist?' In G. Mair (ed.), *What Matters in Probation*. Cullompton: Willan Publishing.

Farrall, S. (2007). 'Desistance studies vs. cognitive – Behavioural therapies: Which offers most hope for the long term'. In R. Canton & D. Hancock (eds), *Dictionary of Probation and Offender Management*. Cullompton: Willan Publishing.

Farrall, S., Bottoms, A. & Shapland, J. (2010). 'Social structures and desistance from crime'. *European Journal of Criminology*, 7(6), 546–570.

Featherstone, L. (2008, 29th November). 'Reading the Baby P serious case review'. Retrieved 13th November 2010, from http://www.lynnefeatherstone.org/2008/11/reading-baby-p-serious-case-review.htm

Featherstone, L. (2009, 12th November). 'Serious case reviews – Baby Peter and beyond'. Retrieved 13th November 2010, from http://www.lynnefeatherstone.org/2009/11/serious-case-reviews-baby-peter-and-beyond-2.htm

Feeley, M. & Simon, J. (1992). 'The new penology: Notes on the emerging strategy of corrections and its implications'. *Criminology*, 30(4), 449–474.

Feeley, M. & Simon, J. (1994). 'Actuarial justice: Power/knowledge in contemporary criminal justice'. In David Nelken (eds), *The Futures of Criminology* (pp. 173–201). London: Sage Publications.

Ferguson, H. (2008, 10th December). 'Social workers are better now at child protection'. *The Guardian*.

Ferguson, H. (2010). 'Walks, home visits and atmospheres: Risk and the everyday practices and mobilities of social work and child protection'. *British Journal of Social Work*, 40(4), 1100–1117.

Field-Fisher, T. (1974). *Report of the Committee of Inquiry into the Care and Supervision Provided in Relation to Maria Colwell*. London: HMSO.

Fijnaut, C. (2001). 'Crisis and reform in Belgium: The Dutroux affair and the criminal justice system'. In U. Rosenthal, R.A. Boin & L. Comfort (eds), *Managing Crises; Threats, Dilemmas, Opportunities* (pp. 235–250). Springfield, Ill.: Charles C. Thomas.

Fitzgibbon, D.W. (2007). 'Risk analysis and the new practitioner: Myth or reality?' *Punishment and Society*, 9(1), 87–97.

Fitzgibbon, D.W. (2008). 'Deconstructing probation: Risk and developments in practice'. *The Journal for Social Work Practice*, 22(1), 85–101.

Fitzgibbon, D.W. & Green, R. (2006). 'Mentally disordered offenders: Challenges in using the OASys risk assessment tool'. *British Journal of Community Justice*, 4(2), 35–46.

Fitzgibbon, W. (2009). 'Mentally disordered offenders in England and Wales and the parole process'. *European Research Institute for Social Work Web Journal*.

Fitzgibbon, W., Hamilton, C. & Richardson, M. (2010). 'A risky business: An examination of Irish probation officers' attitudes towards risk assessment'. *Probation Journal*, 57(2), 163–174.

Fitzgibbon, W. & Lea, J. (2010). 'Police, probation and the bifurcation of community'. *Howard Journal of Criminal Justice*, 49(2), 215–230.

Fletcher, H. (2010). 'Welfare cuts plans flawed Napo warns'. *Napo News*, 225 (December), 5.

Foster, J. (1990). *Villains: Crime and Community in the Inner City*. London: Routledge.

Franklin, B. & Parton, N. (1991). 'Media reporting of social work: A framework for analysis'. In B. Franklin & N. Parton (eds), *Social Work, the Media and Public Relations*. London: Routledge.

Franklin, M. (2004). *Voter Turnout and the Dynamics of Electoral Competition in Established Democracies since 1945*. Cambridge: Cambridge University Press.

Froggett, L. (2002). *Love, Hate and Welfare: Psychosocial Approaches to Policy and Practice*. Bristol: The Policy Press.

Fulwood, C. (2010). 'Criminal justice and New Labour: A personal valediction'. *Probation Journal, 57*(3), 286–290.

Furedi, F. (2007). 'From the narrative of the blitz to the rhetoric of vulnerability'. *Cultural Sociology, 1*(2), 235–254.

Garboden, M. (2010). 'Gove reveals how £670m will be cut from children's services'. *Community Care*. Retrieved 21st November 2010, from http://www.communitycare.co.uk/Articles/2010/06/08/114672/gove-reveals-how-670m-will-be-cut-from-childrens-services.htm

Garland, D. (1985). *Punishment and Welfare: A History of Penal Strategies*. Aldershot: Gower.

Garland, D. (2001). *The Culture of Control: Crime and Social Order in Contemporary Society*. Oxford: Oxford University Press.

Gentleman, A. (2010, 29th October). 'Minister calls for more child protection volunteers'. *The Guardian*.

Gill, C., Slack, J. & Fernandez, C. (2009, 5th June). 'Families of French students tortured by psychopath to sue British authorities for failing their sons'. *The Mail*. Retrieved from http://www.dailymail.co.uk/news/article-1190498/Families-French-students-Laurent-Bonomo-Gabriel-Ferez-tortured-Dano-Sonnex-sue-British-authorities.html#ixzz11ssav14G

Gillen, S. (2008, 16th January). 'Progress on Lord Laming's key proposals from the Victoria Climbié report'. *Community Care*.

Glancey, J. (2006, 6th November). 'Brave new world'. *The Guardian*.

Goodman, A. (2003). 'Probation into the millennium; the punishing service'. In M. Roger & J. Young (eds), *The New Politics of Crime and Punishment*. Cullompton: Willan Publishing.

Greer, C. (2011). *Crime News*. London: Routledge.

Gregory, M. (2010). 'Reflection and resistance: Probation practice and the ethic of care'. *British Journal of Social Work, 40*(7), 2274–2290.

Guardian Reporter (1973a, 17th November). 'Maria's care was "beyond her mother"'. *The Guardian*.

Guardian Reporter (1973b, 6th December). 'Maria case social worker "showed perseverance"'. *The Guardian*.

Hall, C., Parton, N., Peckover, S. & White, S. (2010). 'Child-centric Information and Communication Technology (ICT) and the Fragmentation of Child Welfare Practice in England'. *Journal of Social Policy, 39*(3), 393–413.

Hall, S., Winlow, S. & Ancram, C. (2008). *Criminal Identities and Consumer Culture; Crime, Exclusion and the New Culture of Narcissism*. Cullompton: Willan Publishing.

Hallett, C. (1983). 'Social workers: Their role and tasks (1982)'. *British Journal of Social Work, 13*, 395–404.

Hammerton, A. (1992). *Cruelty and Companionship: Conflict in Nineteenth-Century Married Life*. London: Routledge.

Hannah-Moffat, K. (2005). 'Criminogenic needs and the transformative risk subject: Hybridisation of risk/need in penality'. *Punishment & Society, 7*(1), 29–51.

Hansard (2009). 'Sonnex case. Commons Debates, 8 Jun 2009: Cols 517–519'. Retrieved 14th July 2009, from http://www.publications.parliament.uk/pa/ cm200809/cmhansrd/cm090608/debtext/90608-0004.htm#0906083000165

Hansard (2010). 'Probation officers: Working hours'. *Written Answers and Statements, 22 October 2010: Cols 909W–910W.* Retrieved 14th December 2010, from http://www.publications.parliament.uk/pa/cm201011/cmhansrd/ cm101022/ text/101022w0002.htm#1010227000081

Hanvey, C. (2003, 13th February). 'The blame cascades down'. *Community Care.* Retrieved 25th September 2010, from http://www.communitycare.co. uk/Articles/2003/02/13/39653/The-blame-cascades-down.htm

Haydon, H. (2008, 16th November). 'YOU have made your voices heard in the fight for justice for Baby Peter'. *The Sun.*

Hesketh, J. & Hewett, P. (1972). '100 probation breakdowns and the concept of failure'. *British Journal of Criminology, 12*(4), 390–399.

Hier, S.P. (2003). 'Risk and panic in late modernity: Implications of the converging sites of social anxiety'. *British Journal of Sociology, 54*(1), 3–20.

Hier, S.P. (2008). 'Thinking beyond moral panic: Risk, responsibility, and the politics of moralization'. *Theoretical Criminology, 12*(2), 173–190.

Higgs, L. (2010, 26th April). 'Judge warns of Shoesmith fallout'. *Children & Young People Now.* Retrieved 14th November 2010, from http://www.cypnow. co.uk/news/ByDiscipline/Social-Care/999078/Judge-warns-Shoesmith-fallout/

Hill, L. (2009). *Investigation into the Issues Arising from the Serious Further Offence Review: Dano Sonnex.* London: National Offender Management Service.

Hitchens, P. (2008, 15th November). 'If Baby P had been middle-class, he'd have been taken away'. *Daily Mail.*

HM Inspectorate of Probation (2006a). *An Independent Review of a Serious Further Offence Case: Anthony Rice.* London: HMIP.

HM Inspectorate of Probation (2006b). *An Independent Review of a Serious Further Offence Case: Damien Hanson & Elliot White.* London: HMIP.

HM Inspectorate of Probation (2006c). *Joint Thematic Inspection Report: Putting Risk of Harm in Context.* London: HMIP.

HM Inspectorate of Probation (2006d). *"Working to Make Amends": An Inspection of the Delivery of Enhanced Community Punishment and Unpaid Work by the National Probation Service.* London: HMIP.

HM Inspectorate of Probation (2009). *A Stalled Journey: An Inquiry into the Management of Offenders' Risk of Harm to Others by London Probation in: Greenwich & Lewisham; Hackney & Tower Hamlets; Merton, Sutton & Wandsworth; and Brent, Barnet & Enfield.* London: HMIP.

Hobbs, D. (1988). *Doing the Business: Entrepreneurship, the Working Class and Detectives in the East End of London.* Oxford: Clarendon Press.

Home Office (2002). *OASys User Manual v.2.* London: National Probation Directorate.

Home Office (2003). *Managing Offenders, Reducing Crime – Correctional Services Review.* London: Home Office.

Home Office & DHSS (1975). *Report of the Committee of Inquiry on Mentally Abnormal Offenders (Cmnd 6244, Butler Committee)*. London: HMSO.

Home Office, Lord Chancellor's Department & Office of the Attorney-General (2002). *Justice for All (CM 5563)*. London: TSO.

Horsfield, A. (2003). 'Risk assessment: Who needs it?' *Probation Journal*, 50(4), 374–379.

House of Commons Education Committee (2010). *Child Safeguarding: Oral Evidence 15 September 2010. HC 465-i*. London: The Stationary Office.

Hudson, B. (2001). 'Punishment, rights and difference: Defending justice in the risk society'. In K. Stenson & R. Sullivan (eds), *Crime, Risk and Justice*. Devon: Willan Publishing.

Hudson, B. (2003). *Justice in the Risk Society*. London: Sage Publications.

Institute for Fiscal Studies (2010). *Press Release: Child and Working-Age Poverty Set to Rise in Next Three Years (16 December)*. London: Institute for Fiscal Studies.

Jewkes, Y. (2004). *Media and Crime: A Critical Introduction*. London: Sage Publications.

Jones, C. (2001). 'Voices from the front line: State social workers and New Labour'. *British Journal of Social Work*, 31, 547–562.

Kemshall, H. (2003). *Understanding Risk in Criminal Justice*. Berkshire: Open University.

Kinsey, R., Lea, J. & Young, J. (1986). *Losing the Fight Against Crime*. Oxford: Blackwell.

Laming, H. (2003). *The Victoria Climbié Inquiry (CM 5730)*. London: HMSO.

Laming, H. (2009). *The Protection of Children in England: A Progress Report (HC 330)*. London: The Stationery Office.

Latchman, A., Pratt, C. & Trowbridge, M. (1972, 30th June). 'Open door to murder: Storm over the poison boy set free to become a killer'. *Daily Express*.

Lea, J. (1992). 'Left realism: A framework for the analysis of crime'. In J. Young & R. Matthews (eds), *Rethinking Criminology: The Realist Debate*. London: Sage.

Lea, J. (2002). *Crime and Modernity*. London: Sage Publications.

Lea, J. & Young, J. (1984). *What is to be Done About Law and Order? – Crisis in the Eighties*. Harmondsworth: Penguin.

Lebloch, E. & Beresford, P. (2010, 1st December). 'Volunteers must not take the place of professional social workers'. *The Guardian*.

Leeser, R. (2008). *Indices of Deprivation 2007: A London Perspective*. London: Greater London Authority, Data Management and Analysis Group.

Lewis, L. (2005, 3rd November). 'Schoolgirl blogger poisons mother in homage to killer'. *The Times*. Retrieved from http://www.timesonline.co.uk/tol/news/world/article585815.ece

Lister, R. (ed.) (1996). *Charles Murray and the Underclass: The Developing Debate*. London: Institute of Economic Affairs.

Littlechild, B. (2008). 'Child protection social work: Risks of fears and fears of risks – Impossible tasks from impossible goals?' *Social Policy & Administration*, 42(6), 662–675.

Lloyd, A. (1995). *Doubly Deviant, Doubly Damned*. Harmondsworth: Penguin Books.

London Probation Board (2009). *Annual Report 2008/9*. London: Ministry of Justice.

Lynch, M. (2000). 'Rehabilitation as rhetoric: The ideal of reformation in contemporary parole discourse and practices'. *Punishment & Society*, *2*(1), 40–65.

Mackie, L. (1973, 10th October). 'Child who died told neighbour: "Don't let me go back"'. *The Guardian*.

Maier, E. (2008). 'Baby P: The story of Haringey whistleblower Nevres Kemal: Nevres Kemal alleged bad practice in Haringey in 2004'. *Community Care*.

Mair, P. (2006). 'Ruling the void: The hollowing of Western democracy'. *New Left Review*, 42.

Malone, C. (2008, 16th November). 'Baby P: They're ALL guilty'. *News of the World*.

Marquand, D. (2004). *The Decline of the Public: The Hollowing Out of Citizenship*. Cambridge: Polity Press.

Maruna, S. & Immarigeon, R. (eds) (2004). *After Crime and Punishment*. Cullompton: Willan Publishing.

Maruna, S., Porter, L. & Carvalho, I. (2004). 'The Liverpool desistance study and probation practice: Opening the dialogue'. *Probation Journal*, *51*(3), 221–232.

Masson, J. (2006). 'The Climbie; Inquiry – Context and critique'. *Journal of Law and Society*, *33*(2), 221–243.

Maynard-Moody, S., Musheno, M. & Palumbo, D. (1990). 'Street-wise social policy; resolving the dilemma of street-level influence and successful implementation'. *Western Political Quarterly*, *43*, 831–846.

McCulloch, T. & McNeill, F. (2007). 'Consumer society, commodification and offender management'. *Criminology and Criminal Justice*, *7*(3), 223–242.

McIntosh, F. (2009, 7th June). 'The British justice system is a disaster… God help us 'cos we know Gord can't'. *The Mirror*.

McLaughlin, K. (2006). 'Regulation and risk in social work: The general social care council and the social care register in context'. *British Journal of Social Work*, Advanced access 10.1093/bjsw/bcl079.

McNeill, F. (2006). 'A desistance paradigm for offender management'. *Journal of Criminology and Criminal Justice*, *6*(1), 39–62.

Mead, G. (2006). 'History of Whitehawk'. Retrieved 25th October 2010, from http://www.mybrightonandhove.org.uk/page_id_6907_path_0p114p462 p1242p.aspx

Milner, J. & O'Byrne, P. (1998). *Assessment in Social Work*. Basingstoke: Palgrave.

Ministry of Justice (2009). *Offender Management Caseload Statistics 2008*. London: Ministry of Justice.

Ministry of Justice (2010). *Offender Management Caseload Statistics 2009: An Overview of the Main Findings*. London: Ministry of Justice.

Minton, A. (2009). *Ground Control: Fear and Happiness in the Twenty-First-Century City*. London: Penguin Books.

Mowlam, A. & Creegan, C. (2008). *Modern-day Social Evils: The Voices of Unheard Groups*. York: Joseph Rowntree Foundation.

Munro, E. (2004). 'The impact of audit on social work practice'. *The British Journal of Social Work, 34*(8), 1075–1095.

Munro, E. (2009). 'You've told them what to do Lord Laming – Now explain how to do it'. Retrieved 3rd August 2010, from http://www.parliamentary-brief.com/2009/03/youve-told-them-what-to-do-lord-laming-now-explain

Munro, E. (2010a). 'Learning to reduce risk in child protection'. *British Journal of Social Work, 40*, 1135–1151.

Munro, E. (2010b). *The Munro Review of Child Protection. Part One: A Systems Analysis*. London: Department for Education.

Murray, C. (1984). *Losing Ground*. New York: Basic Books.

Nash, M. & Williams, A. (2008). *The Anatomy of Serious Further Offending*. Oxford: Oxford University Press.

Nellis, M. (2004). 'The electronic monitoring of offenders in Britain: A critical overview'. In Julian Buchanan & et al. (eds), *Electronic Monitoring of Offenders: Key Developments*. London: NAPO ICCJ Monograph.

Nellis, M. (2007). 'Humanising justice: The English probation service up to 1972'. In L. Gelsthorpe & R. Morgan (eds), *Handbook of Probation* (pp. 21–58). Cullompton: Willan Publishing.

Neustatter, A. (2008, 12th November). Too easy a target. *The Guardian*.

NSPCC (2008a). *A Pocket History of the NSPCC*. London: National Society for the Prevention of Cruelty to Children.

NSPCC (2008b). *Evidence to Lord Laming's Review of Child Protection*. London: NSPCC.

Ofsted (2007). *Annual Performance Assessment of Services for Children and Young People in the London Borough of Haringey*. London: Ofsted.

Ofsted, Healthcare Commission & HM Inspectorate of Constabulary (2008). *Joint Area Review. Haringey Children's Services Authority Area*. London: Ofsted.

Oldfield, M. (2002). *From Risk to Welfare: Discourse, Power and Politics in the Probation Service*. London: NAPO ICCJ Monograph.

Ooms, T. (2002). 'Strengthening couples and marriage in low-income communities'. In A. Hawkins, L. Wardle & D. Coolidge (eds), *Revitalising the Institution of Marriage for the Twenty-First Century: An Agenda for Strengthening Marriage*. Westport CN: Praeger.

Parton, N. (1985). *The Politics of Child Abuse*. Basingstoke: Macmillan.

Parton, N. (2004). 'From Maria Colwell to Victoria Climbié: Reflections on public inquiries into child abuse a generation apart'. *Child Abuse Review, 13*, 80–94.

Parton, N. (2008). 'Changes in the form of knowledge in social work: From the "social" to the "informational"'. *British Journal of Social Work, 38*, 253–269.

Peelo, M. (2006). 'Framing homicide narratives in newspapers: Mediated witness and the construction of virtual victimhood'. *Crime Media Culture, 2*(2), 159–175.

Penna, S. (2005). 'The Children Act: Child protection and social surveillance'. *Journal of Social Welfare and Family Law, 27*(2), 143–157.

Phillips, M. (2008, 16th November). 'The liberals who did so much to destroy the family must share the blame for Baby Peter'. *Daily Mail.*

Platell, A. (2009, 6th June). 'Two brilliant students and our feral underclass'. *Daily Mail.*

Prins, H. (1999). *Will They Do It Again? Risk Assessment and Management in Criminal Justice and Psychiatry.* London: Routledge.

Pritchard, C. & Williams, R. (2010). 'Comparing possible "child-abuse-related-deaths" in England and Wales with the major developed countries 1974–2006: Signs of progress?' *British Journal of Social Work, 40*(6), 1700–1718.

Probation Association (2010, September). 'Minister engages with trusts to help them grasp "greatest opportunity in 100 years"'. *Probation Association News Update.* Retrieved from http://www.probationassociation.co.uk/media/8920/pa%20news%20update%20sept%202010.pdf

Proops, M. (1973, 29th November). 'Marjorie Proops talks to Sir Keith Joseph'. *Daily Mirror.*

Ramsbotham, D. (2009, 9th June). 'The probation service sham'. *The Guardian.* Retrieved from http://www.guardian.co.uk/commentisfree/2009/jun/09/probation-service-bureaucracy-sonnex-scott

Roberts, R. (1973). *The Classic Slum: Salford Life in the First Quarter of the Century.* Harmondsworth: Penguin.

Robinson, G. (2003a). 'Risk and risk assessment'. In W.H. Chui & M. Nellis (eds), *Moving Probation Forward* (pp. 108–129). London: Pearson.

Robinson, G. (2003b). 'Implementing OASys: Lessons from research into LSI-R and ACE'. *Probation Journal, 50*(1), 30–40.

Robinson, G. (2005). 'What works in offender management?' *The Howard Journal, 44*(3), 307–318.

Robinson, G. & Burnett, R. (2007). 'Experiencing modernization: Frontline probation perspectives on the transition to a National Offender Management Service'. *Probation Journal, 54*(4), 318–337.

Rodger, J.R. (2008). *Criminalising Social Policy: Anti-social Behaviour and Welfare in a De-civilised Society.* Cullompton: Willan.

Rolin, H. (1976). 'The care of the mentally abnormal offender and the protection of the public'. *Journal of Medical Ethics, 2,* 157–160.

Ross, B. (Writer) (1995). *The Young Poisoner's Handbook.* UK: British Screen Productions.

Scott, D. (2009, 10th June). 'Arrested development'. *The Guardian.*

Scott, D. (2010). 'Who's protecting who?' *Probation Journal, 57*(3), 291–295.

Sennett, R. (2010, 30th July). 'The ASBO is an icon of New Labour's negligence'. *The Guardian.*

Shaw, I., Bell, M., Sinclair, I., Sloper, P., Mitchell, W., Dyson, P., et al. (2009). 'An exemplary scheme? An evaluation of the integrated children's system'. *British Journal of Social Work, 39*(4), 613–626.

Siddique, H. & Jones, S. (2008, 11th November). 'Two men found guilty of causing Baby P's death'. *The Guardian.*

Simon, J. (2007). *Governing Through Crime.* Oxford: Oxford University Press.

Smith, D. & Stewart, J. (1997). 'Probation and social exclusion'. *Social Policy & Administration, 31*(5), 96–115.

Squires, P. & Stephen, D. (2005). *Rougher Justice: Anti-social Behaviour and Young People*. Cullompton: Willan Publishing.

Tobin, L. (2010, 8th November). 'G4S cuts cost of contracts to win government'. *Evening Standard.*

Tomes, N. (1978). 'A torrent of abuse: Crimes of violence between working class men and women in London 1840–1875'. *Journal of Social History, 11,* 328–345.

Tran, M. (2009, 8th June). 'Straw blames probation management over French students' murder'. *The Guardian.*

Travis, A. & Gillan, A. (2009, 4th June). 'Killers of French student pair jailed as Jack Straw apologises for blunders'. *The Guardian.*

Trotter, C. (1999). *Working with Involuntary Clients: A Guide to Practice*. Sydney: Allen & Unwin.

Trotter, C. (2004). *Helping Abused Children and Their Families*. Sydney: Allen & Unwin.

Trotter, C. (2009). 'Pro-social modelling'. *European Journal of Probation, 1*(2), 138–148.

Tunstill, J. (2007). *Volunteers in Child Protection*. London: Community Service Volunteers.

Tweedie, N. (2008, 15th November). 'Haringey: Where no one will hear you cry'. *Daily Telegraph.*

UNISON (2008). *Still Slipping Through the Net? Front-Line Staff Assess Children's Safeguarding Progress*. London: Unison.

Valios, N. (2010, 16th July). 'Pros and cons of using volunteers in child protection'. *Community Care.*

Vanstone, M. (2004a). *Supervising Offenders in the Community. A History of Probation Theory and Practice*. Aldershot: Ashgate.

Vanstone, M. (2004b). 'A history of the use of groups in probation work: Part two – From negotiated treatment to evidence-based practice in an accountable service'. *Howard Journal of Criminal Justice, 43*(2), 180–202.

Vanstone, M. (2010). 'New Labour and criminal justice: Reflections on a wasteland of missed opportunity'. *Probation Journal, 57*(3), 281–285.

Vigarello, G. (2001). *A History of Rape: Sexual Violence in France from the 16th to the 20th Century*. Cambridge: Polity.

Wacquant, L. (2007). *Urban Outcasts: A Comparative Sociology of Advanced Marginality*. Cambridge: Polity.

Wacquant, L. (2009). *Punishing the Poor*. Durham NC: Duke University Press.

Walker, D. (1973, 3rd November). 'Donald Walker reports on the case which has shocked Britain'. *Daily Mirror.*

Walklate, S. (1998). 'Crime and Community: Fear or Trust?' *British Journal of Sociology, 49*(4), 550–564.

Ward, V. (2008, 14th November). 'Baby Peter: Mother's sick online boast'. *Daily Mirror.*

Warner, J. & Gabe, J. (2006). 'Risk, mental disorder and social work practice: A gendered landscape'. *British Journal of Social Work, Advance Access doi: 10.1093/bjsw/bcl334.*

Watford Observer (1972). 'Graham Young, the Bovingdon poisoner'. *The Watford Observer*. Retrieved 15th August 2010, from http://www.watford-observer.co.uk/nostalgia/crimelibrary/grahamyoung/thebovingdon-poisoner/.

Watts, B. (2008). *What are Today's Social Evils? The Results of a Web Consultation*. York: Joseph Rowntree Foundation.

Webb, S. (2006). *Social Work in a Risk Society: Social and Political Perspectives*. London: Palgrave Macmillan.

White, S., Hall, C. & Peckover, S. (2009). 'The descriptive tyranny of the common assessment framework: Technologies of categorization and professional practice in child welfare'. *British Journal of Social Work*, *39*(7), 1197–1217.

Willmott, P. & Young, M. (1960). *Family and Class in a London Suburb*. London: Routledge & Kegan Paul.

Wilson, W. (1987). *The Truly Disadvantaged*. Chicago: Chicago University Press.

Winnett, R. & Porter, A. (2010, 20th October). 'Spending Review 2010: Axe to fall on half a million public sector jobs'. *Daily Telegraph*.

Wise, S. (2008). *The Blackest Streets: The Life and Death of a Victorian Slum*. London: Bodley Head.

Wood, H. & Lynch, D. (2009, 4th June). 'Inside the horror flat where two French students were tortured and murdered'. *The Mirror*.

Wood, J. & Kemshall, H. (2007). *The Operation And Experience of Multi-Agency Public Protection Arrangements (MAPPA)*. London: Home Office.

Wrennall, L. (2010). 'Surveillance and child protection: De-mystifying the Trojan horse'. *Surveillance and Society*, *7*(3/4), 304–324.

Young, J. (1987). 'The tasks facing a realist criminology'. *Contemporary Crises*, *11*, 337–356.

Young, J. (1992). 'Realist research as a basis for local criminal justice policy'. In J. Lowman & B. MacLean (eds), *Realist Criminology: Crime Control and Policing in the 1990s*. Toronto: University of Toronto Press.

Young, J. (1999). *The Exclusive Society: Social Exclusion, Crime and Difference in Late Modernity*. London: Sage Publications.

Young, J. (2003). 'Merton with energy, Katz with structure: The sociology of vindictiveness and the criminology of transgression'. *Theoretical Criminology*, *7*(3), 389–414.

Young, M. & Wilmott, P. (1962). *Family and Kinship in East London*. Harmondsworth: Pelican.

Index